Dare to be Different

Dare to be Different

Bill Bright

Kim Twitchell

CHRISTIAN FOCUS

Copyright © 2004 Kim Twitchell
ISBN 1-85792-945-4
Published in 2004 by
Christian Focus Publications
Geanies House, Fearn,
Ross-shire, IV20 1TW,
Great Britain
www.christianfocus.com
email: info@christianfocus.com

Cover design Alister Macinnes
Cover Illustration Pete Roberts
Printed and bound in Great Britain by
Cox & Wyman, Reading.

Cover illustration depicts Bill Bright sharing *The Four
Spiritual Laws* with a young student on campus as part of
his ministry with Campus Crusade for Christ.

For Ethan, Ben, Grace, Douglas Jr.,
Peter, Cole, and Jack.

Your great-grandmother, Beryl Dee, once said
she frequently prayed for the next seven
generations of her family. You have been
prayed for, and are loved dearly.

Contents

Growing up in Oklahoma

Laced-up boots kicked up clouds of dust along the long stretch of road. A round-faced, brown-haired boy hastened ahead of his brothers and sisters who fanned out along the lane behind him, each carrying a satchel of books. They laughed and their voices floated up into the breeze.

The young boy stooped to pick up a rock. He threw it down the lane. The Oklahoma afternoon sun beat down. A light breeze rustled across the plains. It swirled the dust in the path ahead. But the sun and the dust went unnoticed. The boy sighted a lone figure coming toward him. Squinting, he peered down the lane. He grinned. It was Mother.

'Bill!' she called, waving. Then she greeted each of her children as they, too, rushed toward her, 'How was your day?' she queried of each child, 'What did you learn?'

The Bright family lived on a ranch five miles from the little town of Coweta, Oklahoma and for the next two miles, before they arrived home, lively conversation filled the otherwise lonely road. Eleven-year-old Bill Bright and his four brothers and two sisters told their mother, Mary, of the day spent in a rural, one-room schoolhouse. As Bill's brothers and sisters pushed forward with their mother in animated conversation, Bill's pace slowed down so he could have some thinking time to himself. He kind of wished he could spend the afternoon back at the old frog pond - even in the height of summer he could still imagine the snow and ice covering everything, icicles hanging off trees, snowballs flying through the air, sledding down the hill behind the barn. And ... then ... just behind a grove of trees and within range of the school bell, Bill had discovered the most wonderful thing of winter – skating!

Thump! Startled, Bill's mind left the pond. His brother, wearing an impish grin, had knocked Bill's books off his shoulder. Sprinting past Bill toward the rambling two-storey white house now looming ahead, he turned back to yell, 'Last one to the barn does all the chores!' But it was always the case that all the Bright children did their fair share of household work - race or no race.

Changing quickly into farm clothes, Bill joined his brothers at the barn. They cleaned the barn and milked the cows. 'Hey Bill,' one of his brothers called, 'Meet you at the corn crib!' Hanging up the final pails and rakes, Bill met his brother at the old corn-crib now falling into disrepair. Selecting corn silks from a pile on an old crate, Bill's brother rolled a cigarette for Bill. Then, for himself, he selected brown peach leaves and rolled his own cigarette. Coughing from their first puffs, the boys grimaced. 'This tastes awful!' said Bill. 'Yeah,' agreed his brother. But neither boy put his cigarette down. It made them feel grown-up ... like their father, Forrest Dale Bright. After the first few splutters, the boys leaned back and gazed off at the sun. It lingered just a few feet from the tips of the waving golden wheat.

'Tomorrow will be a big day,' Bill mused out loud. It was June – harvest time for winter wheat. After days of combining, they were finally finishing up the last field. Bill loved the sight of the golden fields waving in the purples and oranges of the setting sun. He loved it almost as much as the smell of new-mown hay or the fruit trees newly budded in the spring.

All of the children were expected to help with the harvest, as well as with the chores on the 5,000-acre ranch. Tomorrow, they would help the men bring in the rest of the wheat. Other Saturdays were spent repairing fences, driving the herds to pasture, and cleaning out the barns. It wasn't all just hard work though. They had fun times too. Bill had just learned to ride his father's horses bareback. He hoped his father would soon let him ride bronco-style too.

But Oklahoma in the 1930s meant hard work for most folks. Days after Bill's eighth birthday, New York's Wall Street stock market crashed, and people were suddenly out of work. Even though New York was 1,700 miles away from the ranch, Bill could tell that things had changed. His father referred to it as the 'Great Depression.' Families lost their homes and followed the crops looking for work. Many lived out of their cars. And when Bill went to town with his father, he saw people standing in bread and soup lines.

Bill's grandfather, Samuel, had been a pioneer in the oil business and was very successful. While many families lost everything, the Brights still had food on the table and clothes on their backs. Bill's mind went back to yesterday when they had passed a traveling black family on the road. The father politely asked Mrs. Bright for directions to town. They were looking for work, he told her.

As the family walked down the dusty road, Mrs. Bright sighed at the disappearing figures. 'We have great privilege. We have been given much by God. Never forget that. You are no better than anyone else. Never look down on someone because of the color of his skin,' she warned.

The two brothers puffed their last puffs on their makeshift cigarettes and Bill rose to his feet. 'Let's go in. I want to finish my homework before supper.'

11

Dare to be Different

Mrs. Bright bustled between the stove and the dinner table, while Bill worked on his homework. The smell of fresh baked bread wafted to where he and his brothers lay sprawled in the parlor with piles of books around them. Bill reached for his favorite magazine, anxious to finish just a page.

'Bill, Glenn, Forrest, Dale!' Mrs. Bright called, gathering her family to the table. Reflecting her German heritage, it was customary for Mrs. Bright to serve her husband and her children first, wait upon them during the meal, and eat later. As the Bright family gathered around the table, Mrs. Bright noticed there was still one empty spot. With a sigh and a twinkle in her eye, Mrs. Bright hastened to the door of the parlor. There he was, still enraptured by the magazine story before him.

'Bill,' she whispered into the now emptied room, with an understanding smile. She loved to read as well, and Bill, more than any of her other children, was a dreamer like her. His mind would fly away to an imaginary world as fast as her own. But, her husband would be hungry and the food was getting cold.

'Bill!' she called louder this time, turning to hasten back to the dinner table, 'It's time for dinner. Don't make your father wait!'

After dinner, with the dishes cleared and washed, the family gathered in the parlor once again. Each evening, the children would gather before the fireplace to listen to Mrs. Bright read from her favorite classics. Before marrying Dale Bright, Mary Lee Rohl had been a schoolteacher in Indiana. Her cousin was the popular poet James Whitcomb Riley, whose poems they read on occasion. But tonight, they were reading the exciting adventures of Achilles in *The Iliad*.

Mrs. Bright, seated close to the fire, read out in a clear voice and Bill began to think about the characters he was hearing about. 'Achilles' mother must have been beautiful,' he thought as he gazed at his own mother by the fire. 'Surely, she was as beautiful as my mother.'

Bill could never remember his mother being angry with the children. She disciplined them, spanked them even, but not in anger. She did not criticize, but often reached out in kindness. Their neighbors frequently turned to her when ill or in need, for she was known for her compassion. Their ranch had become a social center for their disheartened community. Many would come for homemade ice cream or watermelon socials. Others would come to ask Bill's father, Dale, for advice about cattle.

'Time for bed!' The call broke Bill out of his thoughts. He scurried up the stairs after giving his mother a kiss. Tomorrow was a big day, he remembered, as he pulled his nightshirt on.

Hours before sunrise, Bill woke to the sound of his father's stomping into the kitchen with a fresh pile of wood for the fire. Bill and his brothers hastened to find their socks and working clothes. Scrambling down to the kitchen, the boys quickly ate breakfast, eager to get their chores out of the way. Then, they could help with the harvest. Bill's mother, her braid of hair not yet pulled up into her bun, winked at her boys as they raced out to the barn.

A cluster of men emerged from the early morning mist and prepared to help Bill's father bring in the last of his harvest. 'There might be a treat toward the end of the day,' Forrest whispered to Bill. 'Father might bring out that wild bronco he just brought in and try to break him, if we get the harvest in fast!' he finished excitedly.

Bill's face broke out into a grin. No one was a better rancher than his father, he thought, Father could ride the wildest horses and steer[1] – he had a gift with animals.

'My father goes into a corral of wild horses,' bragged Bill to his schoolmates one day, 'and they just tremble.' Bill trembled a bit, too: His father had a will of steel. And, while he was never abusive, he had a temper. Bill knew that if his father's voice was raised, he ought to obey, no questions asked. Dale Bright's strong will was best seen when he was breaking in a new bronco. It was wise, Bill and his siblings learned early on, not to disagree with their father. Their neighbors learned it as well. Bill's father counted on the honesty of men, often transacting large business agreements and sealing the deal with nothing more than a word over a handshake.

But Dale Bright's strong will was part of what made him successful in conquering this western territory. And Bill wanted to be like his father.

The harvest day passed quickly and soon, the last of the wheat was cut. Bill's father made arrangements for his new threshing machine to be sent over to his neighbor's farm a few weeks later. Sharing resources and caring for others was a lesson Bill learned at an early age.

Bill leaned over the fence. He listened as Mr. Bright showed his neighbor the machine. His father might be a bear of a man, thought Bill, but he was kind in his own way.

Mr. Bright noticed the line of boys hanging off the fence with pieces of straw clenched between their teeth and simply jerked his head to the right. It was their cue to get off the fence. As they jumped down, Mr. Bright then nodded to the barn. Wide smiles appeared on each boy's face. It was time to let out the broncs! As the boys ran to the paddock, their shouts

14   [1]Steer - another word for Cattle, oxen etc.

of glee floated along the breeze. For the rest of the afternoon, the children watched their father try to break the bronco, finally seating him as the sun began to set in the west.

After the excitement died down, Bill grabbed the pitchfork to clean out the stalls in the barn. Inside the quiet of the stable, he walked over to his own horse, whom he had named Pet. Reaching into his pocket, he pulled out a carrot and pushed it up to the horse's mouth. 'Hey there,' Bill whispered. 'Don't you worry,' Bill continued, 'I still like you best over that new bronco. Maybe we'll get to ride tomorrow.'

Riding Pet was one of Bill's favorite things. Bill was learning the whole length of the ranch – all 5,000 acres. He and Pet would often gallop across the prairie. There seemed to be no end. Bill sighed. 'Maybe tomorrow,' he whispered.

After dinner, Bill's mother reminded the children that baths must be taken that night. 'Church tomorrow,' she called as she headed to the kitchen to boil water. The boys grimaced. 'We are going to Grandfather Bright's house for dinner afterwards, so you will need to be extra clean,' she finished. Bill looked down at his hands. He knew his face must also reflect a day spent in the fields. Sure enough, evidence of the hard day's labor floated by Bill in the tub that evening while he was scrubbed. But soon enough the scruffy little farmhand was all pink and fresh. Bill then headed off to bed, for a night filled with dreams of wild bronco riding.

The next morning, after chores and breakfast, Bill and his brothers and sisters dressed in their best clothes before heading into town with their mother and father. Arriving at the Methodist Church, Bill watched his father say goodbye. Mr. Bright went to join several townsmen to talk politics and business. Church was for women and children, Bill had heard his father once say to his mother.

As soon as the service was over, Bill and his siblings raced to find their father, to begin the fifty mile drive to their grandfather's house. Bill could not wait to see his grandparents. He was in awe of Grandfather Samuel Bright, who had even been elected mayor of the town.

One of Bill's favorite memories was during last year's summer trip. His grandfather had taken him into town on a business errand. Before they left, Grandfather Bright handed Bill a store-bought ice cream cone at the town drugstore! He knew his grandson had a sweet tooth.

'Incredible,' Bill thought, feeling the cold ice cream slide all the way down to his stomach. But there was a warm feeling in Bill that day too. He felt extra special all day.

Now, with the harvest cut, Bill's parents decided it was a good time to visit the senior Brights. Would cousins be there, the children wondered? What treats would Grandmother Bright have in her kitchen? What new games would she have? Excitement grew with each passing mile. Soon, the house loomed into view.

'Welcome, dear ones!' Grandmother Bright called from the porch. She was elegant with perfectly groomed light brown hair and a warm smile. She reached out to hug each child as they scampered up to meet her. She was always warm and loving, so Bill thought her to be the best grandmother anyone could have. Every child was important to her. She just made him feel like he belonged, thought Bill.

Wide-eyed, Bill and his brothers and sisters stepped into the house and eagerly looked around. The floors were so polished Bill could see his face in them. And the bearskin rugs! Bill had never seen bearskin rugs until he came to Grandfather Bright's house!

A tall, impressive figure with a regal appearance stepped from the fireplace, beaming at his family pouring into the room. Grandfather Bright made quite a figure with his own elegant manner.

'Welcome!' he greeted them, crossing the room to shake hands with Bill's father and kiss Bill's mother lightly on the cheek. 'Greetings to all of you, you Bright children,' his voice sang musically, turning to greet the seven children, each in turn. 'Are you hungry? Dinner is ready, I believe.'

Over steaming piles of mashed potatoes, a roast chicken, gravy, beans, and freshly-baked bread, Bill's father and grandfather discussed their latest business ventures and talked politics. The children listened quietly. They knew this was not the time to speak. Bill's father talked about the harvest and the bronco he had worked with. Grandfather Bright leaned forward, anxious to hear the story. 'Ah, it's been too long,' he sighed with a faraway look in his eye.

After a moment of silence, Bill timidly spoke up.

'Grandfather,' Bill queried, 'Will you tell us again the story of how you came to Oklahoma?'

With eyes twinkling, the imposing man laughed heartily for a moment.

'Well, Bill, didn't I tell you that story the last time you visited?' his grandfather teased.

'Yes...' said Bill, blushing now.

'Oh, please, Grandfather! Do tell us! You must tell us!' came a chorus of voices from around the table. As Bill's brothers and sisters clamored for the story, Grandfather winked at Bill. Regaining his confidence, the eleven-year-old joined in with his brothers and sisters.

'Well, there's not much to tell,' Grandfather Bright began. The lilt in his voice suggested quite the opposite. 'Oklahoma was known as Indian territory in 1889. The United States government wanted men and women to settle the land and they were willing to give the land away in land grants. And so, in the years between 1889 and 1895, they had great land-grant rushes. I was a schoolteacher,' Grandfather Bright continued, glancing at Bill's mother with another wink, 'but I wanted adventure! So, I saddled up my trusty horse one fine spring day, went to the land-grant office and signed up to "make the run."'

Grandfather Bright picked up his glass as if he were done with the story. He leaned back in his chair, seemingly content with the amount of information he had given.

Voices clamored again: 'What happened then? Grandfather, you can't stop there! Tell us about the run!'

Chuckling, Grandfather Bright closed his eyes. He seemed to go through a catalog of memories in his mind. Then he opened them, having selected just the perfect one.

'We all lined up. Each of us held stakes with flags. We were to ride out to the land we wanted, and drive the stake into the land we were claiming. Now, as we waited for the race to start, some of the horses were more skittish than others. And some folk, ... well ... some folk had hardly ridden a horse in their lives. There were wagons, even a bicycle or two. Women and men lined up. Some of the wagons had children hanging out of them! But there was one thing we all had in common,' Bill's grandfather paused as he surveyed his grandchildren's faces, 'We all had fierce determination. We were going to get some land!'

Telling the story spurred on his own excitement.

'Crack!' he yelled out. The children all jumped. They

did it every time, even though they had heard the story often. Thrilled expressions appeared on the boys' faces, while the girls recovered more slowly from their shock. 'The pistol was fired! We took off … hundreds of horses lunging forward! My neighbor … Mr. Whippenstead … well, his horse reacted poorly to the pistol. He reared up and turned around. But my neighbor held on for dear life! I don't know much of what happened to him after that since my horse took off at a gallop. We closed the distance on those in the lead pretty quickly.'

Grandfather Bright leaned closer to the table. 'Now,' he whispered looking into each child's eyes, 'I had spied out the territory the week before. I knew where I wanted to claim my land. I saw two other riders ahead of me, and so I dug in, urging my horse forward with everything he had.' Grandfather Bright's voice grew louder and faster with each sentence. 'I chased those two riders like a dog chasing a rabbit.'

Giggles erupted around the table, but quickly quieted.

'Before I knew it, I had moved ahead of the first rider. Gallop! … Gallop!' Grandfather Bright punctuated the story with sounds. 'I crossed the hill where your barn sits now. Gallop! Now, I was on the piece of land I had wanted. Gallop! Gallop! Before that first rider came over the hill, I jumped off my horse!'

Grandfather Bright's eyes gleamed. 'I nearly broke my leg, jumping off a galloping horse! I tumbled to the ground. But I got right up, picked up my stake and thrust it straight into the soil! Exhausted, I collapsed. Riders whisked past me. I could see their frowns and heard … well, let's say colorful language!' He glanced apologetically at Grandmother and Mrs. Bright and then chuckled, 'It was pretty tense for a minute there. I wasn't sure if they were going to pull out pistols on me or not!'

Seeing concern flash in his granddaughters' eyes, he laughed loudly and quickly added, 'But they did not. They moved on to the next piece of property. And so that is how your old grandfather "made the run" and helped settle this great state of ours,' he finished. 'And,' he added, 'I made friends with the two riders who became neighbors that day. We have remained friends to this day.'

Bill knew that once the competition for the land was over, his grandfather had exhibited the same behavior he witnessed in his own father. Community and shared resources were more important than competition. Once, Bill learned, his grandfather had convinced a group of men to invest in oil property that did not turn out as well as he had hoped. His grandfather refunded the men's money with a loss to himself. His grandfather was an honorable man.

Later that afternoon, as Bill and his family left to go home, Bill gazed back at his grandparent's house for as long as it was in sight. With such a heritage of courage and honesty and strength, Bill thought, there was much expected of him. Could he be brave like his grandfather? Or like his father riding the bronco? Would he have the courage to do something like 'make the run'? Would he be compassionate like his mother? What territory was out there that he could claim? What stories would he have for his grandchildren some day?

Finding a Voice

Standing before a sea of faces, Bill could not remember ever being this nervous, not even on the wildest bronc in his father's paddock. A trickle of perspiration gathered on his forehead. Bill reached for the handkerchief his mother had given him as they left the house that morning.

'You might need this,' she had whispered, placing it in Bill's hand and then giving him a quick hug. Bill reached up, patted his forehead, and promptly put the cloth back into his pocket.

Bill had been selected to give the eighth grade graduation speech. He had been so excited and spent hours preparing in the barn. Now, gulping, his excitement was like a runaway train.

With resolve, Bill stood taller and, ignoring the snickers coming from the front row of Bright siblings, began his prepared speech. With each sentence, he gained confidence, silencing the front row. In what seemed like a flash, he was done. Stepping away from the podium, Bill descended the stairs. Pulling out the handkerchief, he again patted his forehead, slowly becoming aware of the sound of clapping.

After the ceremony, Bill stood near the punch bowl with his mother and father. To his surprise, parents, classmates, teacher, and even siblings came over to congratulate him on a job well done. 'You sure can give a good speech, Bill!' one of his brothers told him, before running off to steal another cookie from the refreshment table.

Bill took the comment to heart. Perhaps he could explore other opportunities in high school, he thought. But summer was ahead – not much time to worry about that now!

Hard work shaped Bill's summer. Driving cattle, mending fences, feeding livestock and helping in the fields kept him and his brothers busy. But Bill found a few hours each week for fun like riding bareback, and playing football with his brothers out in the newly-cut grass.

As Bill grew taller that summer, so did his opportunities. For the first time, much to his mother's dismay, his father allowed him to ride a wild steer. That evening, at the dinner table, Bill displayed a red and purple bruise swelling on his forehead. He proudly and dramatically recounted the story of his triumph over the steer. Horror reflected in his sisters' eyes. Repeatedly, they glanced up to his bruise. Amusement and pride gleamed in his older brothers' eyes. They seemed to think the egg-size bump more of a trophy.

As Bill continued to speak, his parents looked at each other over the heads of their children. Concern radiated from Bill's mother as she broke away to return to the kitchen for another cold compress for Bill's head. A twinkle appeared in Bill's father's eye.

Before Bill knew it, the sounds of the end of summer traveled on the evening breezes. The hum of the grasshopper-like cicadas rubbing their wings together grew louder. Graduation from the one-room schoolhouse now meant Bill was headed off to the larger school. One evening Bill leaned back and wondered what high school would be like. What would he get involved in?

Bill quickly discovered the Debating Club. To his delight, he enjoyed it and did very well. Bill also joined the football team, despite only being five-foot-six and 125 pounds.

Freshman year of high school seemed a triumph for Bill until one particular afternoon of football. He did not know that that day would change the course of his life.

It was a sunny Saturday. In the midst of a heated game on the football field, Bill found himself in the path of a six-foot, 250-pound fullback bearing down on him like three crazed steers. Despite being half the weight of the fullback, Bill's strong will and determination urged him on. Bill made the quick decision to tackle this giant, with great hopes of stopping him. With a lunge, Bill collided with him.

Wham! Thud.

Something went immediately wrong. The hard-kicking legs of Bill's opponent had not stopped until they met the left side of Bill's skull. Two hundred and fifty pounds slammed into Bill's head, bursting his eardrum. As he was being carried off the field, his father, who had been watching the game in the stands, met him. His face told Bill all he needed to know. Normally a man of great humor, the look on his father's face told Bill he would not be playing football anytime soon.

Weeks after the game, Bill slowly healed. Having no other significant injuries Bill was heartbroken not to be able to play. Sitting in the stands watching from the sidelines grew to be too much for Bill. He pleaded with his father to let him return to the game. But Mr. Bright remained resolute.

Bill knew not to cross his father. He had been raised to be obedient. So he searched out other activities to busy himself. Before long, he had found what seemed the perfect solution – combining both his love for sports and his talent for public speaking. Bill got quite a name for himself when he became the announcer for the football team's home games.

While Bill began high school, his father began to take a greater role in politics, becoming the chairman of the Republican Party for their county. Candidates for all kinds of positions were invited to Coweta to speak – from those running for governor of the state of Oklahoma to those hoping to represent the county in Congress in Washington, D.C. As Bill's talent as an announcer developed, he was invited to become the master of ceremonies for political events. Bill was soon meeting men of prominence from all over the state of Oklahoma.

Visitors often shared meals with the Bright family and discussed politics. As a result Bill learned much about government and how it contributed to society. Just two years earlier, President Roosevelt had introduced the 'New Deal,' a plan for the government to help feed and clothe its citizens. It was hoped it would go some way towards helping people get back on their feet after the Great Depression. Bill was discovering the value of a commitment to community and shared resources. He listened with increasing interest.

Throughout Bill's time in high school, J.J. and Alice Woolman, a successful and energetic couple, were regularly invited to join the Brights. The Woolmans owned the weekly newspaper, *The Coweta Times-Star*. During one such supper visit, Mr. Woolman turned to Bill.

'Bill,' he began, smiling, 'You are doing a fine job announcing the football games, and at your father's rallies.' Mr. Woolman offered a nod of approval at Mr. Bright, before returning his gaze to Bill.

Sheepishly, Bill looked down at his plate, and mumbled a 'Thank you.' Despite his public speaking, Bill didn't like to be put on the spot. At times, he felt like he could try anything. At other times, he felt very shy.

'Bill,' continued Mr. Woolman, immediately aware of Bill's discomfort, and suddenly very businesslike, 'I would like you to consider writing in the paper for me. You can start by reporting on activities at the high school. What do you think?'

'Mr. Woolman,' Bill stuttered, unsure of how to respond to this exciting opportunity. His heart pounded. Then, just as quickly, memories of his recent struggles with writing flooded his mind. His face flushed. 'I am afraid, sir,' Bill admitted, 'that when I write a letter or essay, I find myself thinking a long ways ahead of my writing. It results in some very poorly constructed sentences.'

Mr. Woolman studied Bill for a moment. With a quiet voice, Mr. Woolman cleared his throat, drawing Bill's eyes up from the table to him.

'Bill, I appreciate your honesty. I believe that is exactly the kind of reporter I am looking for to write for the newspaper,' he continued, waving away Bill's objections. 'Tell you what we will do. We will work on your "poorly constructed sentences" together. Communication is critical, Bill, in whatever venture you pursue. Learning how to communicate takes time.' Mr. Woolman paused, allowing the words to settle on Bill.

'Do we have a deal?' he asked the young man.

A smile slowly stretched across Bill's face.

'Yes,' he said quietly. Then, more excitedly, words bubbled forth. 'Thank you, Mr. Woolman!' Bill exclaimed, 'I promise I will do my best! And thank you again, sir!'

With that settled, Bill began reporting on school activities, often staying up late the night after the weekly football game, recounting the play-by-play action of his fellow classmates. Before Bill knew it, his writing was improving under Mr. Woolman and his journalists' watchful eyes. Racing home one afternoon, Bill thought his heart would jump out of his chest with pride.

'Mother!' he called as he ran up the driveway, 'Mother!'

Bill's mother hurriedly appeared at the front door, soapy water dripping from her hands as Bill bounded up the porch steps, two at a time. 'You'll never guess!' Bill panted. 'Look,' he said excitedly, pointing to page one of *The Coweta Times-Star*. There, under a bold headline she read the words, 'by William R. Bright.'

'A front page article, Bill!' she exclaimed, beaming. 'Oh, Bill, I am so proud!' Hugging her son, Mrs. Bright told him, 'Your father is mending the southwest fence today. You must go show him!' Bill scampered down the stairs, eager to show his father his latest accomplishment.

By the time Bill finished high school, the list of his accomplishments had grown. Determined and self-sufficient, he took on many challenges and even joined the drama team. Bill was the lead in two high school plays during his senior year. He organized a 4-H club, an organization for high school students, teaching them to be productive and responsible citizens. Soon, Bill was elected president of the club, and won several awards. He became business manager of the high school paper and the yearbook. And he continued to write for *The Coweta Times-Star*.

In addition to the hard work he had put in on his father's ranch, Bill grew his own herd of registered shorthorns. He was elected president of the Future Farmers of America in North Eastern Oklahoma. He was proving to be a good rancher. In fact, he was pocketing prize money at livestock judging contests throughout the state, taking some of the highest honors.

He was also receiving honors for his public speaking and it was becoming evident that there was something special about this young high school student. The title of one speech was 'I Dare You.' Standing tall, this now lean, dark-haired, handsome young man leaned forward and challenged the farmers in front of him to use various methods of soil rotation to enhance their land's use. 'I dare you to be different!' he challenged them, 'Every farmer is a fool ...' he punctuated his last word, pausing dramatically, waiting for the full import of the words to take effect, ' ... who stands by year after year and watches his soil wash away without doing anything about it!'

Bill had courage and the strength to be different ... something that would stand him in good stead at other points in his life. But for now his strength was focussed on his own ambitions.

By the time graduation arrived for the High School Class of 1939, Bill had excelled in academics, student government, drama and debate and had become quite an accomplished orator. During rare moments of quiet inactivity, sitting and watching the sun sink into the wheat-fields, Bill thought about his future. He decided he wanted to be a rancher, go to law school, own a newspaper, and later go into politics, maybe even run for Congress. For the moment, his immediate plans included studying economics and sociology at the state college in Tahlequah, Oklahoma.

On the night of his high school graduation, Bill, was once again selected to give the class oration. It was the perfect end to Bill's high school career. The next edition of *The Coweta Times-Star* reported that Bill's speech, 'The Hope of Democracy,' had been well-delivered by that year's winner of the 'Best All-Round Student' award.

Unbeknownst to Bill, one particular seventh grade girl sat in the back of the room, listening intently to his speech. Her name was Vonette Zachary. She sat with her father, Roy Zachary, a respected businessman in the community, who owned the town's main service station. Impressed with Bill's well-prepared speech, she watched with attentiveness as he received his 'Best All Round Student' award. Suddenly aware that she had been staring at Bill Bright, Vonette glanced quickly at her father, wondering if he had noticed her particular interest. Assured he had not, Vonette settled back in her chair. Watching Bill Bright once more, the young girl smiled.

Westward Bound!

The early autumn breeze tickled the checkered curtains and whispered a change in the season. The tan, lean young man shuffled some papers into a pile, resting a freshly written list on top of a pile of books. Bill's trunk sat open on the floor. Clothes and a few toiletries, not yet packed, rested in a pile next to a suitcase on the bed.

The list was private, not meant for anyone else's eyes but his own. Bill had spent a last few moments writing down goals for his university days: to graduate with honors, to be elected class president, editor of the yearbook, student body president, and much like high school, the university's most outstanding student.

Bill's mother entered the room. In her arms was the last of the fresh laundry just plucked from the line. Quickly, Bill hastened to put the list away. To some, he reasoned, the list would look arrogant. To him, the goals were stepping stones to further career objectives.

Bill's mother put the laundered clothes on the bed. Bill smiled and thanked her. As he turned back to his desk to slip a piece of paper into a book, Mrs. Bright sighed. 'I'm going to miss you, Bill,' she said simply as she left his room. Bill looked after the retreating figure, with a sudden ache. It wasn't as bad as when his mother had left him at the one-room schoolhouse many years ago. Then he had cried. But he would miss his mother fiercely, he thought. She really was a saint.

Bill left next morning for university. He waved until the figures in front of the ranch house could not be seen any more. Sadness competed with excitement as he turned around in his seat. Finally, looking forward, excitement won out. The forty-mile road to Tahlequah from Coweta was symbolic. It became littered with everything Bill was leaving behind – small town life, the monotony of familiar places, even the simple fencings of his religious upbringing. A new beginning was ahead, he thought. His goals became his life's purpose. With such plans, he figured he could change the world.

Bill stayed true to his course. He studied public speaking, drama, and debate, became the yearbook editor, was elected class president, and later student body president. He excelled in his classes and would be selected as the college's most outstanding student. But despite his accomplishments, Bill remained an intriguing mix of determination and shy hesitancy. He still did not like being put on the spot, nor did he like being conspicuous before crowds.

In fact, one evening during his college career Bill was asked to make an announcement at a college basketball game. As student body president, it was part of his responsibility. When the players finished the quarter, Bill eyed the forty foot distance between his seat and the podium.

'I'll be right back,' he told his friend who had joined him to watch the game. Bill stood, but moved in the opposite direction from the podium. Confused, his friend called after him, 'Bill, where are you going? The podium is this way!' he exclaimed, pointing in the opposite direction from the retreating figure. Shortly, Bill re-emerged on the other side of the podium, several feet closer than if he had walked from his seat. Realizing that Bill had just walked around the building to get to the podium, his friend shook his head, smiling. Next to the long list of Bill's accomplishments, his shyness was perplexing.

'Bill!' Bang! Bang! Bang! 'Bill!'

Bill got up from his chair. He looked at the clock. It was 2:00 p.m. on what had been an otherwise peaceful Sunday afternoon. Who would be banging on his door so urgently on a Sunday?

Bang! Bang!

It was the first week of December in Bill's junior year. The students were in the middle of writing papers and taking final exams. Bill was studying for an exam that next day.

'Bill!' the shouts continued, 'They've bombed Pearl Harbor! Bill, did you hear me? We're at war!'

By the time Bill got to his door, his friend had raced into the staircase to continue to broadcast his announcement. Bill stood at his door, taking in the news. Questions flooded his mind. Who had bombed? What was bombed? What had happened?

By evening, Bill's questions began to find answers. The Japanese government had launched a surprise attack on the United States Naval fleet at Pearl Harbor, in Oahu, Hawaii. Thousands had died. It was only a matter of time now before the United States declared itself at war.

It took less than twenty-four hours. The next day, President F.D. Roosevelt declared that the United States was, indeed, at war. Passion exploded in Bill's chest. It wasn't a question. He would fight to defend his country. He would enlist immediately. Joining the river of faces that flooded out the doors of the local Selective Service office, Bill peered anxiously ahead. His friend was emerging from the building.

'They aren't taking college students yet,' he called to Bill, disappointedly.

Bill turned out of line, disappointed as well.

Later that night, after many discussions with friends on what to do, Bill had resolved to push through the rest of college as quickly as he could. Much like pushing through unwelcome chores on the ranch, Bill would move forward with great drive and determination. Real life, the defense of his country were now the most important. Real life was now on the front lines in the Pacific and in Europe.

With renewed energy, Bill attacked his obligations with new vigor. For the next year nothing could stop Bill's ambition.

The Coweta Times-Star would report Bill's progress twelve months later in the midst of his senior year. He had become president of the student body at Northeastern State College. He was president of his fraternity[1]. He was the editor of the college yearbook. The list went on and he also continued to receive awards as a speaker. For the next six months, Bill studied hard and won the Most Outstanding Student award. But for Bill all that graduation meant was that he could finally serve in the military. He wrote to West Point and to the Naval Academy. It had been a long year, but he was close to achieving his goal – to join his three brothers and many of his fellow students defending their country.

'I'm sorry, Mr. Bright.'

The words clattered his hope to the floor.

'What do you mean, sorry?' Bill's question echoed in the hollow of the hall outside the army doctor's office.

'You have failed your physical examination, Mr. Bright. And I cannot, therefore, recommend you for active duty,' the doctor finished.

32 [1]A group of usually male students, like a university club.

'Surely you were aware that your perforated eardrum would be a factor?' the doctor asked.

'But it is only my ear! I am in fine physical condition otherwise!' Bill countered, growing angry, 'What does my eardrum matter? I can hold a weapon. I grew up on a ranch – I can shoot better than the last three men who came in here! I can strategize. I can lead men! How can my ear matter so much when thousands of men are dying!'

Shrugging weakly, the doctor nodded. 'I understand. But the Germans are using poison gas.' Turning back to finish the paper work, he finished, 'It would kill you immediately with your ear the way it is. It is too great a risk.'

Kicking the curb as he left the doctor's office, Bill's mind went back to that football field eight years ago. The injury had now ruined a year-long dream as well as football.

'Oh, to get a hold of that 250-pound fullback now!' he muttered, clenching his fists. His feet pounded the road, frustration working its way out with each stride.

Bill's back straightened as he continued his walk home. The discouragement seemed to fade with each stride. By the time Bill arrived in his room he was resolved to seek other avenues. Someone will take me into the military, he thought to himself, confidence now replacing frustration. This was just a glitch, he mused, pulling out pen and paper at his desk. Sitting down, he began to plan out his strategy.

'I can appeal the decision,' he thought to himself. 'If that doesn't work, then I can talk to my friends at the draft board[2]. Maybe they can help me?' He scribbled down the names of friends to contact. 'And if that doesn't work, I can take the exam in Oklahoma City.'

But despite Bill's persistence, the same answer came back over and over. No.

[2]These officials organised military applications during war time   33

Incredibly discouraged, the newly graduated young man returned home instead of being shipped overseas. He was to help his father on the ranch. With his brothers and a brother-in-law off to the war, his father needed his help. But despite the long hours of hard labor and heavy responsibility, Bill felt unproductive. The war was all that mattered.

Not accustomed to failure, he continued his battle. He tried the Air Force, then, the Marines. He even tried the Coast Guard. Turning to his father's political connections, Bill had written to the top national Republican leader as well as future president and Democrat Harry Truman who was chairman of the special Senate committee and analyzing the country's war effort. But the answer remained the same. No.

Driving into town for a rare break from his chores and responsibilities, he pulled over at the sight of streamers and waving crowds. Stopping a neighbor, Bill asked what the excitement was all about.

'One of Coweta's own has come home,' the neighbor beamed proudly, holding up a newspaper article before thrusting it into Bill's hands. He turned up the road to the gathering crowd. 'What a record!' he called back, over his shoulder, 'Thirty-one bombing missions, a Distinguished Flying Cross, four Oak Leaf Clusters and a Purple Heart!'

Bill peered over the article. His heart pounded with an unfamiliar ache. What was that he felt? Anger? No, Bill realized. Anger disguised envy: men were returning from a war that he was forbidden to enter. It just wasn't fair.

Throwing his vehicle into gear, Bill backed away from town to return to the farm, his face flushed red. The rejection stung. This was the first thing he had not been able to accomplish in his lifetime. Somehow, he just had to get involved in the war, he determined.

Bill decided to apply for a job at the local radio station as an announcer. At least there, Bill reasoned, he would be able to report on the war. Before he began, however, he was offered a teaching appointment with Oklahoma State University. 'Faculty in the field,' was the description of the position – teaching young men wherever they worked – farms, stores, and factories – to increase productivity. What appealed to Bill was that it was supposed to increase productivity for the war effort. He took the job.

One year later, however, the job's potential charm had left. Their lessons over with for the day, Bill's students pushed collectively toward the door and back to their jobs. 'Like a herd of steer heading out of the paddock for the open plain,' Bill observed to himself, as he watched the young men leave. It was 1944 now. He should be pleased with the job, he thought, his cheeks suddenly pink with the idea that ingratitude might be at work in him. He did appreciate the job, he thought with a sigh, but he longed for more.

As he closed up his own satchel of books, he sat back in his chair and gazed out the window. It was almost as though he could see the bombs dropping on the U.S. Navy's ships and planes at Pearl Harbor just three years ago. The dream was still there. Of late, he had begun to realize that he needed to take one more shot, or else replace this dream with another.

His restlessness had been growing. For several months, he had been considering the idea of moving west to California to try entering the military out there. Increasingly, Los Angeles looked appealing. Maybe he had been rejected because he was in a small town, he thought. At the very least, he mused, if he was rejected again, perhaps he could try his hand at making money, or perhaps use his talents to get involved in theatre.

Before long, Bill handed in his resignation at Oklahoma State, had packed up his belongings, said goodbye to his mother and father and was driving west through the American southwestern desert.

On his first night in Los Angeles, Bill thought he would go stir crazy just sitting in his room. He was just twenty-three years old, lean, athletic, and handsome – the spitting image of the movie star, Clark Gable, some thought.

The suitcase lay on the bed, half unpacked. A new Bible peeked out from under a pile of clean shirts. His mother had snuck it in when she helped pack his suitcase before he left Coweta. But Bill barely glanced at it. Certainly, he had no intention of reading it.

His mother's faith had been observed by Bill, but not embraced by him.

At the age of sixteen, Mary Lee Bright had become a believer in Jesus Christ at the Methodist church she attended. She carried that faith forward in her life. Often, Bill saw her rise from kneeling in prayer in her bedroom before the rest of the family was up at 4:00 a.m. for chores. Her Bible would lay open on the bed.

She had almost died when she was pregnant with Bill. Before Bill, his mother and father had lost a baby in childbirth. When Bill's mother became pregnant with him, the doctor told her that her own life was at risk. There was little hope that both she and Bill would live.

When she told Bill the story, she added that she had prayed fervently for both of them. But what Bill did not know was that Mrs. Bright had also asked God to allow Bill to know Jesus Christ as she did. She committed her son to God, and continued to pray for him.

Despite his mother's example, it was his father's attitude toward religion he adopted and when Bill discovered that the pastor in their church had cheated on his wife and left his family in a divorce, Christianity was soured for him. Bill was convinced it had little to offer. He was happy anyway. He had been instilled with good qualities – he was hard working, kind, and had good morals – and he had big plans.

Bill put down his comb and grabbed his keys. Saying goodnight to the elderly couple with whom he was staying, Bill got in his car, and pulled out of the driveway. He had decided to visit the Pasadena Playhouse. After driving for several miles, Bill saw a hitchhiker and engrained with good Oklahoma neighborliness, Bill pulled over to offer him a lift.

As they talked, Bill learned that the young man was a member of the Christian young people's group, the Navigators. In fact, he lived with the Navigators' founder, Dawson Trotman. Before getting out of the car, he invited Bill to join them for dinner. Since he knew no one else in California, the offer was tempting. Bill accepted. Before he knew it, he was being welcomed warmly into the Trotmans' home. Later that evening, the Trotmans invited Bill to join them at a birthday party. It was being thrown for Dan Fuller, a young serviceman recently home from the Navy.

Bill did not know that Dan Fuller was the son of the radio evangelist, Charles E. Fuller. Bill had never heard Mr. Fuller's program, 'The Old-Fashioned Revival Hour.' If he had, he might not have taken the Trotmans up on their invitation. But meeting a radio personality intrigued Bill, as well as meeting a serviceman recently home from the war.

He accepted the invitation, intrigued as well by the Trotmans' intellect and poise. They were unlike any Christians he had ever known.

His first night in Los Angeles had been wonderful, Bill thought later as he readied for bed. Surprisingly, it had not been what he had expected. He had spent the night with Christians.

Shortly after arriving in Los Angeles, Bill appeared before the draft board. Yet, again, he was told he had flunked his physical. Bill appealed the decision. With nothing to lose but his dream, Bill begged the doctor to reconsider. Even if he passed the draft board in L.A., he was told, somewhere down the line, he would be rejected. His last ditch effort was to sign a waiver, but the military refused to accept it and closed its doors once more to Bill Bright.

Bill realized he needed to move forward. After a brief job working for a corrupt ship builder, he learned of a partnership in a speciality foods company. Bill soon realized that his partner was not interested in working hard – not like Bill. He wanted the business to succeed, but his partner was slowing him down. Bill approached his partner with an ultimatum: Either work, buy me out, or let me buy you out. To Bill's delight, his friend sold him his share of the business. Bill immediately changed its name to *Bright's Epicurean Delights*. Bill had a sweet tooth, so he put it to work. He offered candy and confections that just melted in the mouth. He found fruit of the most delectable colors and tastes, including exotic varieties. And he offered delicious jams and jellies that could be used for brunch or high tea. He focused on selling his treats to the rich and famous. Two more lines of products appeared in future years: *Bright's California Confections* and *Bright's Brandied Foods*.

True to his upbringing, it was not unusual for Bill to be at work before the sun rose, and long after the sun set. But his hard work was paying off. The best national stores soon carried his speciality foods. His products were carried in Los Angeles, Dallas and New York by stores such as Bullock's, Neiman-Marcus and B. Altman. As his business grew, so too, did his list of business contacts who formed mentoring relationships with the budding entrepreneur.

But, much like on the ranch, hard work was often accompanied by fun activities. Bill took advantage of being in Hollywood, and studied drama at the Hollywood Talent Showcase. On Sundays, he tried his hand at developing an amateur radio program in the morning, after which he would go horseback riding in the Hollywood hills.

Times were good, he realized one Sunday afternoon as he returned home from a particularly exhilarating ride. He was happy. Money filled his pockets for nice clothes and good cars. He was meeting interesting people, and making many business contacts. He was able to pursue his passions, like theatre and radio. And he especially enjoyed riding. Clumping up the stairs in his riding boots, he realized the next day was Monday. Even as the thought was realized, satisfaction filled him. It was satisfaction that came from hard work done well. Just then Bill's thoughts were interrupted by someone calling his name.

Turning, Bill saw that it was his landlords, an elderly couple who had taken an interest in him since he had arrived. They had repeatedly invited him to join them at their church, First Presbyterian Church of Hollywood, just down the street. 'You will love our pastor,' they had told him, 'His name is Dr. Louis Evans.'

Seeing that they were dressed in their church clothes and were obviously on their way to the evening service, Bill suddenly became very aware that he must smell like the horse he had been riding. Bill politely said hello, but backed away, afraid he might share the smell of stables and sweat with the couple.

'Oh, Bill,' they laughed, 'Don't worry about your clothes. You are fine. We just wanted to invite you to join us. How fortunate that we bumped into you now! The service begins in twenty minutes. We would love for you to join us!'

Bill thanked the couple, but declined the invitation. He should bathe, he told them, before sitting next to them on a pew. Still laughing and calling out to him that it really didn't matter, the couple moved out of the front door. Watching their retreating figures, Bill suddenly decided on a whim to see what this church was like. He could sit in the back away from people, he realized, and slip out before the service ended. And so, still smelling like the stable, Bill Bright walked to the church and crept into the back row by himself.

Before the last hymn was finished, Bill was on his way home. He had tried it, and that was that, he thought.

As Bill walked home, the elderly couple moved down the church's aisle in search of Miss Henrietta Mears[3]. They wanted to talk to her about Bill. Soon, Bill's name was added to a list of young people to be invited to join Miss Mear's college and career group.

The following week, Bill received a call from a young woman from the church's young people's group, inviting him to a party. It was to be held at the ranch of a movie star, she explained. Bill liked the sound of the young woman's voice. Hoping to meet her, Bill accepted the invitation.

40   [3]Read about Miss Mears in Ten Girls Who Changed History

Not everything in Bill's life was turning out the way he had thought. There was much that made him happy. He loved his work, his horse rides, and meeting new people. But he also experienced disappointment and frustration. He was certainly on an adventure.

Little did Bill know that the adventure had just begun. He would soon meet a woman who would change his life forever.

Meeting Miss Mears

The lights flickered across the field from the barn. As Bill crossed the road toward the party the sound of music wafted out. He was surprised to hear a rumble of what seemed to be hundreds of voices.

'There must be 300 people here!' he thought, as he walked past car after car toward the barn.

Striding up the ramp, Bill paused in the frame of the barn doors, opened wide for the occasion. The sight amazed him. Before his eyes were hundreds of the most handsome college-age men and women he had ever seen. A hearty laugh from a young woman three feet in front of Bill suddenly broke his daze. Happy conversation filled the room. Laughter and shouts of glee flooded over him. Bill realized that his jaw had dropped momentarily. He quickly closed it. Spotting the punch table, Bill entered the barn and moved across the wide-planked floor. Accepting a glass of punch from a smiling young woman, Bill smiled in response. He turned to observe the group.

Bill stared, amazed. Christianity as he knew it had only been for women like his mother, and for children. He didn't know any men who had embraced religion – certainly his father had not. The picture before him was intriguing. Christianity in these clothes looked almost fun, he thought.

Before Bill had finished his glass of punch, several young men pulled up beside him to get punch. With great friendliness, they introduced themselves, and pulled Bill into conversation. When people passed or approached the group, they introduced him to even more people. As they talked, Bill realized that he had a lot in common with them. They, too, had goals and ambitions. They knew where they were going. They were intelligent, thoughtful, and well spoken.

Before leaving, Bill had been invited to join his new acquaintances at the next college and career meeting at the church. He was also invited to attend a young businessmen's meeting. Perhaps he would go, Bill thought, as he got into his car.

One meeting led to the next. Soon, Bill found himself a regular attendee of the college and career group. He heard singing that stirred him. He listened to stories of things God had done in people's lives, and was moved, despite his internal struggle. Then, Miss Mears would stand to give a message out of the Bible. After that, there was time to meet and socialize with his new friends.

Surprised at first that a woman led such a group, Bill soon discovered Henrietta Mears was a gifted teacher. In fact, that was what the group called her: 'Teacher.'

She was a natural actress. Small in stature, but vivacious in personality, determined in purpose and always full of good humor, Henrietta Mears commanded attention when she entered a room. Behind thick cut glasses, her eyes sparkled. Spontaneity and creativity characterized her life and flowed into her lessons.

Miss Mears loved life. She had traveled around the world, and seasoned her talks with memories of riding elephants or rickshaws, visiting grand palaces or the poorest of the poor. As much as she loved life, she loved Jesus Christ more. Combining both this zest for life and a passion for Christ, she inspired those who sat in her class.

Miss Mears had come from Minnesota. The high school chemistry teacher had decided to take on a fledgling young women's Sunday school class in her spare time. By the end of the year, 250 high school age women were studying with her. Ten years later, 3,000 young women had sat in Henrietta Mears' Sunday school class. Through prayer, Miss Mears began to sense that God wanted her to focus not on chemistry students, but on young Christian leaders. She was to teach them to reach the world with the gospel of Jesus Christ. It was not long after that realization that Henrietta received a call from a pastor at First Presbyterian Church in Hollywood, California. Stories of her 'spare time' activity had reached his ears, he told her. They needed someone like her to lead their Christian Education department. Would she come? She packed her bags.

This evening her deep, resonant voice echoed in the room. Miss Mears was teaching from her favorite book of the Bible, Romans. 'Paul says that we are not justified by our own works, but by faith in Christ. Now, students, have you been trying to earn God's favor? You can't do it.' She peered into the faces around the room, catching many eyes. 'You must believe in Christ.' She, then, went on to challenge the young men and women to again consider the message of good news about Jesus Christ.

In addition to Miss Mears and the young men and women in her class, Bill began to meet men and women from the church. He had begun to attend the worship service, and had to admit that what senior pastor Dr. Louis Evans taught was intellectually stimulating. All of Bill's oratory training immediately recognized a gifted orator when he heard one. His landlords had been right about Dr. Evans speaking talent. But, it was more than that. Dr. Evans painted a portrait of

Jesus Christ in the most eloquent ways he had ever heard.

But Bill still sat on the back row. He was still more interested in observing than participating.

At a pool party, Bill first met Elwain Steinkamp. He had invited Miss Mears' class to use his large swimming-pool. Bill discovered that his host was a church elder, but also a prominent businessman in the Bel Air community. The Steinkamp family took an interest in Bill. They often invited him back to their home. Bill was interested in Mr. Steinkamp's success as builder in one of the most prestigious areas of Hollywood. But as Mr. Steinkamp shared his experience with Bill, he also included ideas from the Bible.

'Material success is not where you find happiness,' he told Bill on one such visit. 'Some of the most miserable people in this town are the wealthiest. Jesus Christ is the only way to true happiness.'

Bill went home that afternoon, scratching his head. That attitude didn't make sense. It was contrary to everything Bill had grown up knowing. His father might have laughed in Elwain's face. Certainly, it was contrary to what he was experiencing in his own life now. Money was making his life very happy, he grumbled, still shaken by Mr. Steinkamp's view. He respected Mr. Steinkamp very much. He had everything that Bill wanted. There was no one – well, maybe his mother – who would hold to the same view. But she had never expressed it like Steinkamp just had. Yet, the more Christian businessmen Bill met, the more he saw that Christ really did mean more to them than money or success.

One night, Bill sat on his bed looking up in the closet. There sat the unopened box and Bible that his mother had slipped into his suitcase when he moved to California. He sighed. The more services he attended, and the more Bible classes he went to, the more uncomfortable he became with his lack of knowledge. He realized he now had to investigate the Bible further, if for no other reason than to have semi-intelligent conversations with people.

He pulled the box down, and opened it. The Bible was still pristine, Bill observed. Well, of course it was, he thought, he had never used it. Bill took the Bible out of the box and stared at it, thinking. He finally decided that a study of Jesus Christ seemed the best place to start.

Days of study turned into months. As Bill read through the stories of Jesus' life, he became more and more convinced that Jesus was like no one who had ever lived.

He also began to realize something else. Bill knew he was a good person – his mother had raised him to be a man of integrity. Yet, something was still missing. It began to dawn on Bill that perhaps what made him different from all the Christians he was meeting, was that they had Jesus Christ in their lives. He didn't.

One spring evening in 1945, Miss Mears was teaching at the Wednesday night class. They were studying the story of the apostle Paul and his dramatic encounter on a road to the city of Damascus in Acts 9. Miss Mears told of how Paul was blinded by light from heaven.

'Now see what Paul asks,' Miss Mears cut in at one point in the story, motioning the class to continue reading, 'He asks, "Who are you, Lord? And what will you have me do?"'

Moving to the side of the podium, Miss Mears looked out at them, her eyes flashing behind her glasses as she surveyed the room. 'These are the most important questions anyone can ask,' she stated resolutely. 'The saddest people in the world,' she told her class, 'are those who are not doing what God wants them to do. On the other hand, the happiest people in the world are doing exactly what God wants them to do.'

Miss Mears continued, pointing her finger at the text they had just read, 'Paul thought he was doing what God wanted him to do by persecuting Christians. In reality, he was following after his own goals and ambitions. So, God had to set him straight. And so, here we find him on this road, blinded by light coming from Christ.'

Here it was again, Bill thought, suddenly uncomfortable. It was that same attitude Mr. Steinkamp had about happiness in life, and ultimate goals. Except for his depressing pursuit of the military, Bill had always been a pretty happy guy. But he realized that what both Mr. Steinkamp and Miss Mears were talking about was a happiness not based upon circumstances. Rather, it seemed to steady them. It guided their lives.

Miss Mears closed her Bible. 'I am giving you homework tonight,' she told the class. 'While we might not have had an experience like Paul, still the questions he asks are important. I want you to ask those same questions of yourself: *"Who are you, Lord? What would you have me do?"* Your response matters just like Paul's response mattered.'

Stepping back behind the podium, Miss Mears surveyed the sea of faces before her in the room's stillness. 'I want you to follow this three step plan,' she said, raising a fist, putting a finger up with each point.

'Go home.' The first finger went up. 'Get on your knees.' The second finger joined the first. 'And ask God those two questions,' she finished, raising the third finger to join the other two before closing her hand, and dropping it to her side.

Bill left the class, still gripped by Miss Mears' challenge.

As he walked home, he realized that something had grabbed hold of his heart. Reaching his apartment, Bill understood that he was ready to give his life to God. Everything over the past several months had led to this moment: his study of Jesus' life … the classes taught by Miss Mears … his friendships with Christian businessmen … Mr. Steinkamp's mentoring and challenging comments. Through all of these things, what stood out clearly to Bill was God's love. It was overwhelming to him.

Bill kneeled at his bedside. Closing his eyes, he repeated the two questions Miss Mears had given them: 'Who are you, Lord? What will You have me do?'

Because of his personal Bible study and all he had heard at church, Bill knew that he was praying to Jesus, the Son of God, who had died on the cross for his sins. He knew, because Miss Mears had shared it so often in class, that if he invited Jesus to come into his life as his Savior and Lord, he would. This was that time.

When Bill opened his eyes, nothing dramatic seemed to have happened. He wondered if anything would happen – life felt the same as it had before his prayer of surrender to Jesus. But over the following days and months, Bill began to grow in his new found faith. Something dramatic had happened indeed. He had gone from spiritual death to the beginning of eternal life.

Bill grew in his understanding and awareness of God's love for him. He also, in turn, grew in his love for God. Attitudes began to change. Happiness began to look different. And, Bill began to become more and more aware of what a sinner he was, and what a forgiving Savior Jesus was. Bill knew he would never be the same again.

Becoming Expendable

Bill scribbled furiously. 'Go out into your neighborhood. Tell people about Jesus. Learn how to teach the Bible. Sign up to visit the elderly or help feed those who are hungry.' Miss Mears continued down her list, 'When you teach this class, tell the students about the importance of attending church. Help them to learn what it means to worship God. Teach them how important it is to pray. Ask them to think about traveling outside of the United States to tell people about Jesus. Ask them to consider why it might be important to give some of their money to the church.'

Writing hurriedly, hunched over desks were those students whom Miss Mears had selected to become leaders of the class. When Miss Mears paused, Bill tried to shake the cramp out of his hand. He quickly grabbed up his pen when she began to speak again. Finally, she stopped. She had given her students a complete list of what she considered to be important for them to teach. She took seriously her priorities as a teacher. She hoped her students would make a difference in the world.

Bill Bright stretched his hands in front of him. He stared down at the list.

The past several months had been a whirlwind. Changes on the inside of Bill were slowly beginning to affect the daily choices he made. He was still in the candy business. In fact, the business was growing. He continued to work long, hard hours. He was gaining more business advice from

Christian businessmen. He had expanded his product line and was selling his candy and fruits outside of the United States now. He had more employees. But the real change was that Bill was learning how to be a Christian in business.

Bill had not had a dramatic experience that night he had prayed in his bedroom. But as he looked at the list, it slowly dawned on Bill that his life looked very different now. He was learning how to tell other people about Jesus. He was learning to pray. He was attending church regularly. He was reading and studying the Bible, and what it said was making a difference in his life too. The first Scripture Bill memorized was chapter one of the book of 1 John.

'*But if we are living in the light of God's presence, just as Christ is, then we have fellowship with each other...*' Bill murmured to himself as he drove to work in the morning. '*If we confess our sins to him, He is faithful and righteous to forgive us and to cleanse us from every wrong.*'

Bill thought about what he had learned at church: God was perfect and pure – looking at God was like looking into one of the brilliant white spotlights on one of Hollywood's movie studio lots. In comparison, Bill's heart was black – full of sin. His heart looked all the more black when God's spotlight shone on it. But for those who were Christians, Jesus had stepped between them and God's spotlight. When Jesus did that, Bill could have a relationship with God.

Bill shook his head. 'That was amazing,' he thought to himself.

But Bill also learned that he had a few jobs to do too. He was responsible to live more like Jesus. But Jesus was perfect, and Bill was not. Bill would still sin, and God would see it. But 1 John taught him that when Bill did sin, he was to tell God that his, Bill's, actions and attitudes were wrong. And

God promised to forgive him. Bill also learned that Jesus had left him a helper – someone to help Bill live like Jesus – the Holy Spirit. With the Holy Spirit's help, Bill could live the Christian life.

They were simple ideas: to agree with God and tell him that he, Bill, was wrong in his thoughts, attitudes and actions; to ask the Holy Spirit to help him live the Christian life. 'They are simple ideas,' Bill thought, 'but they change everything, especially how I live.'

These ideas challenged Bill.

Miss Mears invited him to join her regularly so that she could teach him from the Bible, and plan and pray for the class. Bill saw in Miss Mears a profound trust in God. She not only told her class to trust in God, but showed them how to do it. She cast her own cares on God because she firmly believed that He cared for her. Bill sought to follow Miss Mears' model. He prayed. He got to know his neighbors and told them about Jesus Christ. Neighbors prayed and asked Jesus to forgive them and change their lives. As he grew in his knowledge of Scripture, he began to teach.

One spring day, he read the headlines that World War II had officially ended. Bill thought of the irony: here he was now using all of his abilities that he had desperately tried to use in the military. Maybe this was what Miss Mears meant when she talked about being in the center of God's will. He was organizing, strategizing, teaching, debating, speaking, creating, writing, surveying and leading. It wasn't long before Bill was elected president of First Presbyterian Church of Hollywood's College and Career Sunday school class. He had never felt more alive.

Miss Mears' vision also captivated the young man. While

other people may have just seen the four walls in the Sunday school room where she taught, Miss Mears saw the world. Her students would tell the world of Jesus Christ, she was convinced.

'There is no magic in small plans,' she once told them. 'When I consider my ministry, I think of the world. Anything less than that would not be worthy of Christ, nor of His will for my life.'

As Bill took on more and more responsibility in the class, he too began to have dreams of what God could do. One day, after spending time talking to someone about Jesus Christ, Bill began to brainstorm ideas on ways to tell people about the life of Christ. An idea struck him. What about capturing the story on film? With picture films still relatively new, there was only one film about Jesus that he knew of, and that was Cecil B. DeMille's movie, *The King of Kings*, made in 1927. Surely he was in the right town to find a film-maker! Bill began to pray about the idea. Gathering information seemed to be the next step, and so, knowing that Cecil B. DeMille was a Christian, Bill contacted the producer to ask him for his advice.

'I would only produce Christian films if I could,' Mr. DeMille told Bill when they met, 'but I don't have the money.' Bill left his meeting, thinking that perhaps his own business might one day make enough of a profit that he could finance the movie himself. But that would be a long time from now, Bill realized, quickly calculating how many years it might take to build up that kind of equity.

The vision had been born, but it would take thirty years to see his idea on the screen.

Along with a constant flow of new ideas, Bill's thirst for Scripture could not be quenched. The more time Bill spent reading his Bible, the more questions he had. He yearned to know more about God. He wanted to have greater understanding. Perhaps more education was the thing to get? Asking those whom he respected at First Presbyterian Church, he soon learned that if he wanted the best education in the Bible – a seminary education – he must go to Princeton Theological Seminary in New Jersey.

'Across the country,' Bill pondered as he drove home that day. 'Well, the best is the best,' he mused, stopping at a red light and surveying the dashboard of his new Ford. His gaze moved to the top of the maroon hood. His mouth curved into a smile. He appreciated the color, but it was what was under the hood that he best loved. This car was fun to drive. Observing the green light, Bill pulled ahead into traffic. 'I could commute to New Jersey. She would be up to it,' Bill thought, patting the cushion next to him.

But what of the business? He had trustworthy employees who could run things while he was gone, he considered thoughtfully. Now, who might have enough investment in the company to take his place as a manager? Mentally, Bill shuffled through names of people with whom he had developed business relationships. Suddenly, he remembered a businessman from church who had recently invested in Bill's company. His son was looking for work, Bill remembered. Perhaps it would be possible to hire this man's son to handle the day-to-day tasks. Then, he could focus on seminary, and keep the business running!

Bill's heart felt light. The burden of how to manage the business while in seminary just might have been solved. It just might work!

Soon, Bill was shaking hands with his new manager, and was applying to Princeton Seminary for the next term's enrolment. Before he knew it, he was halfway across the United States, driving past wheat and barley fields, with a growing excitement at this next adventure.

***

' … In Jesus' name we pray. Amen.'

Silence greeted the final words of a prayer, spoken by a seminarian whose accent was Korean. Around the room were nine men from all over the world: Korea, Africa, England, and the United States. It was early morning, and these men gathered daily to pray before class.

Stepping outside to cross Princeton's still sleepy campus, Bill gazed again at the beauty of the chapel as he left. A beautiful stone structure with tall cathedral ceilings, the elegant chapel reminded Bill of the holiness of God. His short time here had whisked by. He could not get enough of the whole experience. He prayed with fellow students twice a day, once in the morning, and once in the evening. He carried a full course load of classes, and yet, also managed to join one or two groups in the middle of the day if he could. On weekends, Bill continued habits learned at First Presbyterian. He still went out to meet new people, strike up conversations and talk to them about Jesus Christ. He also taught and preached in various churches surrounding the Princeton campus.

One evening, Bill sat reading. He had lately discovered works by Reverend James Stewart, a passionate writer and New Testament scholar from Edinburgh, Scotland.

If we could but show the world that being committed to Christ is no tame, humdrum, sheltered monotony, but the most thrilling, exciting adventure the human spirit could ever know, those who have been standing outside the church and looking askance at Christ would come crowding in to pay allegiance, and we might well expect the greatest revival since Pentecost.[1]

His heart quickened and the book slipped, falling to his lap. 'That is it, isn't it?' he thought excitedly. He recalled being captivated by the attractiveness of the Christians at First Presbyterian Church in Hollywood. He found that same spiritual charisma, that same social and intellectual appeal here at Princeton. There was something in being able to reflect Christ well. Jesus Christ is appealing – and he does draw men to himself. Most people would say yes to Christ if he was properly and truly portrayed, thought Bill.

Christianity had proven to be everything but humdrum, and Jesus Christ was the reason. The words of Reverend Stewart continued to dance in Bill's head that night as he got ready for bed. He looked in the bathroom mirror and thought again of his public speaking professor's challenge earlier that semester. 'When you step down from the podium,' Bill's professor asked, 'What will people say? Will they say, "What a truly magnificent preacher that young man is!"' the professor had paused and then softly continued, 'Or, will they instead say, "What a great Lord that young man serves." Let that be your challenge.'

The radio sputtered and crackled as Bill drove across hilly plains. He had packed the car and started out on his first cross-country commute back to take care of the business. His plan included stopping in Coweta to see his family. He figured he was but an hour from home now.

Pulling into town, Bill drove past the old Methodist church on his way to the ranch. Much to his delight, he saw a sign in the front of the church. It announced a series of revival meetings that were to take place that week. Bill thought about the revival all the way to the ranch.

Since Bill had become a Christian, his own father's salvation had weighed on him. He had often prayed asking God to change his father. So now that he was home Bill asked his parents if they would go into town to attend the revival meeting with him.

His parents agreed to go.

While the preacher was not eloquent, Bill recognized a simple and deep faith in the man as he spoke. Finishing his sermon, the evangelist invited the congregation to come forward. He urged believers to put their hands on others' shoulders and offer to walk down the aisle with them.

Bill sat still. He didn't know what to do. His father was a proud man. He didn't want to embarrass him. He might never come back to church. But as Bill prayed, asking God for guidance, he soon felt that he was to go over to his father and invite him to the front of the church.

With his heart in his throat, Bill moved over to his father. He asked him to join him.

Dale Bright stood, followed by Bill's mother and walked to the altar. He knelt before the raised step, and leaned forward. But, after a moment, he turned to Bill, who was kneeling beside him. Whispering, he told Bill he wasn't yet ready. He did not want to make a decision for Christ that night.

Bill took his parents home. He said good night and climbed the stairs to his room. Alone, disappointment washed over Bill. His father had been so close. He had had such hopes. Deep down, despite his discouragement, Bill knew ultimately that his father was in God's hands. He sighed. He needed to trust God in this situation.

The next morning after breakfast, Bill casually asked his parents if they would like to return to the revival that evening. Much to his surprise, they both agreed to return. That evening, they drove to town together, found seats, and listened to the preacher. Once again, the preacher asked those listening to come forward to the altar, and to invite someone along. Again, Bill rose and walked over to his father.

Dale Bright stood and accompanied by his wife and son, moved to the altar. Kneeling alongside his father, Bill looked over and whispered, 'Are you ready, Dad?'

The elder Bright looked at his son, a tear shining in his eye. 'Yes, son,' he whispered back, 'I am.'

A few moments later, he stood. But instead of returning to his seat, Dale Bright moved to where another of his sons, Glenn, sat. Recently home from the military, Glenn had joined his family at the revival that night. Dale put his arm around his son, and led him forward. Glenn would not pray that night, but would later receive Christ as his Savior.

For the Bright family, and the townspeople who had known Dale Bright for decades, that memory would forever be one of the most moving.

Bill's two pursuits – seminary on one coast and business on the other – was stretching him beyond what was wise. He soon realized that his business was beginning to suffer because of his lack of attention. What he had hoped would have been a workable situation, was not working. He was needed in California.

Then, Bill learned that Charles E. Fuller, the radio preacher and father of his friend, Dan Fuller, whom he had met on his first night in California, had established a seminary in Los Angeles. He could be one of the first new students.

Bill decided it was too good to pass up. This would allow him to take care of his business while he pursued his degree.

And so, after one year at Princeton, Bill said goodbye and moved back to California.

When Bill returned, Miss Henrietta Mears was herself returning from a trip to Europe now devastated by the recent world war. Anxious to see her, Bill joined Miss Mears at the Forest Home Conference Center in the San Bernardino mountains at a teachers' training conference.

'Europe is in ruins,' she told the group. 'Great is the pain, and great is the need for the love of God in Christ,' she sighed. Bill observed his teacher for a moment, disturbed by her countenance. She was not her normally bubbly self. Miss Mears seemed to have come home wearing the devastation she had found in Europe. It was not long before she was pouring that compassion into messages that declared with new urgency the world's need for Jesus Christ.

Later that night, Bill took a walk. He needed to reflect on her words: *God has an answer. Jesus said that we must make disciples of all men. We are to take His gospel to the ends of the earth. We must become evangelists, even though evangelism is not recognized as a valid program. We must present the full doctrine of Christian truth.*

God is looking for men and women of total commitment. During the war, men of special courage were called upon for difficult assignments; often these volunteers did not return. They were called 'expendables.' We must be 'expendable.'

If we fail God's call to us tonight, we will be held responsible[2] .

As he walked, Bill bumped into Louis Evans, Jr., his pastor's son – now the president of the college and career class at First Presbyterian of Hollywood. He, too, had been reflecting upon Miss Mears' words. Both men decided to visit her. They went off to find her cabin. Soon, the two young men and Miss Mears were in deep conversation.

Before long, all three slipped to their knees in prayer. In what could only be described as an unbelievable experience, Bill felt overwhelmed by the presence of God.

Another young man, also affected by the message that evening, appeared at the cabin door. He, too, quickly joined them on his knees. His name was Richard Halverson, and he was the pastor of a small church in California. Discouraged in his ministry, he had come to seek Miss Mears' counsel, when he was drawn to pray and worship God with the small group. He, too, experienced a change immediately. All sense of discouragement left him.

Their prayers shifted from praise of God to prayers for people who did not know him. They found themselves praying specifically for college students. They prayed for students they knew, but then prayed for students on campuses throughout the United States. Urgency filled the group as they prayed more fervently for these men and women, the future leaders of their generation. Men and women who needed Jesus Christ.

They finished praying. Rising to their feet, everyone pulled chairs into a circle. There was an awareness in each person that something miraculous had just happened. As a group, they had just experienced the overwhelming presence of God. They had also experienced a real desire to give their lives to God to use however he would wish. They discussed things and began to wonder what they should do first.

The group decided they must have a name. 'Fellowship of the Burning Heart!' suggested one young man. 'It comes from John Calvin's seal that shows a hand offering a heart. The inscription reads, "My heart I give Thee, Lord, eagerly and sincerely."'

They thought further. They must be expendable –

available for whatever God would desire them to do, they thoughtfully concluded. After all, it was Miss Mears' words that had brought them to her cabin in the first place.

Leaving Miss Mears' cabin, the three young men moved to one of their cabin rooms, not yet ready for sleep. Deciding to go further, the three men recorded the night's events and wrote out four commitments:

I pledge myself to a disciplined devotional life in which I promise through prayer, Bible study, and devotional reading to give God not less than one hour per day (Psalm 1).

I pledge myself to holy living that by a life of self-denial and self-discipline, I might live out chastity and virtue that will magnify the Lord (Philippians 1:20-21).

I pledge myself to seek every possible opportunity to tell people about Jesus Christ to the end that I may be responsible for leading at least one person to Christ every 12 months (Matthew 28:19; Acts 1:8).

I present my body a living sacrifice, utterly abandoned to God. By this commitment …I offer myself to be expendable for Christ (Romans 12:1-2; Philippians 3:7-14).[3]

As the three men finished, they realized that their lives would never be the same. Expendable for Christ, they hoped. It would change their lives forever.

Vonette Zachary

Bill slowly drove his Ford onto the campus of the Texas State College for Women, in Denton, Texas. He strained to see the building numbers, his fist holding a handwritten note with directions. His car crawling, he finally pulled up to a building that matched the description on the page.

Climbing out of his car, he glanced nervously from the page to the building. He was oblivious to two women students who passed by, giggling and whispering as they raised eyebrows at this handsome stranger in the sporty maroon car.

He took a deep breath and climbed the steps to the front door. Running a finger down the list of names, he stopped at *Zachary, V.* Pulling his handkerchief out of his pocket, he patted his forehead. He pushed the buzzer next to the name. A young woman's voice answered, and told Bill she would be right down.

As he waited for the young woman to emerge, Bill's mind raced back over the events of the past few months that had led to him standing here, that had led to this night.

***

It was one year earlier on a beautiful California summer evening. Bill's younger sister Joann was visiting from Coweta. As a special treat for her birthday, Bill had taken her out to the famous Coconut Grove restaurant at the Ambassador Hotel. Bill knew that movie stars frequented the restaurant and he hoped they might spy someone famous. It would add to the night's festivities and give Jo some great stories to tell when she got back home. They were not disappointed.

As Bill and Jo lingered over dessert, talking and laughing over a childhood memory, Diana Lyn, a beautiful young actress who was very popular, walked by their table.

Jo's eyes lit upon the actress. She could not pull her gaze away, her head slowly rotating as the beautiful woman swished past. Joann giggled, and blushed when, turning, she saw Bill watching her.

'Bill, I could have reached out and touched her!' she laughed. Glancing back at the figure moving elegantly through the crowded restaurant, she remarked, 'She is quite beautiful, isn't she?'

Bill agreed, staring after the young movie star. Suddenly, he sat back, his face scrunched up, his mind obviously occupied by some inner thought.

Jo laughed, seeing his expression. 'What is it, something you forgot to do? Or, is it some new business idea? I swear, Bill, the way you have so many ideas ...' She was stopped in mid-sentence.

'No ...' Bill said slowly, shifting his gaze back to his sister. 'I suddenly realized that she reminds me of someone. I was trying to figure out who...' Realization dawned on Bill's face, and he leaned forward to search his sister's face. 'She reminds me of that Zachary girl back home,' he said. 'You know the one. You are friends with her, aren't you?' he asked his sister, 'She was in your class, I think.'

Bill thought back to his recollections of Vonette. He had met her when she was a little girl, three or four years old. She had attended his mother's Sunday school class at the Methodist Church. Bill also remembered her from high school days and because she had always seemed exuberant, the center of everything.

Suddenly understanding, Jo nodded, with a twinkle in her eye.

'What is she up to now?' Bill asked her, ignoring the playful grin that now stretched across his sister's face.

'Well, ...' Jo replied, slowly, teasing her brother with deliberate slowness. 'She is studying at the Texas State College for Women in Denton, Texas. But, she's home for the summer now.' Impishly, Jo added, once more grinning at her brother, 'I've got her address, if you want it.'

Bill leaned back. Looking at Jo, he smiled. Yes, he did want it.

The next day, Bill brought Vonette's address with him to work. Glancing at his sister's handwritten note several times in the first hour, Bill finally leaned through the office doorframe to tell his secretary that he needed a brief moment to work on a project. He asked not to be disturbed. Closing the door, Bill moved over to his desk. Before sitting down, he opened the drawer and pulled out a sheet of his business stationery. A beautifully scripted letter 'B' graced the top of the page with the words, *Bright's Brandied Foods*.

Sitting down, Bill thought for a moment. How best to impress her, he wondered? Get her attention? Maybe just tell her the truth, he decided. He began to write:

Dear Vonette,

I was having dinner last night with Jo at the Ambassador Hotel, at the Coconut Grove. We saw a beautiful starlet, and she reminded me of you. Hope you're having a good summer.

Signed Bill

Bill put the letter into an equally elegant envelope and addressed it. Pleased with his effort, Bill opened his door, and put the letter on the outgoing mail pile. As he walked back into his office, Bill grinned. He realized he could hardly wait for a reply. But wait was what Bill did.

On a bright sunny Oklahoma morning a few days later, Vonette was handed the elegant envelope. She wondered who would be writing her from California. Remembering her friend, Jo, had taken a trip to visit her brother, Vonette opened the letter, thinking it might be from her.

To her surprise, Vonette glanced at the signature, and realized quickly that it was from Bill, Jo's brother. Vonette felt her face grow warm. She had noticed Bill Bright years ago, sure that he would make something of himself. He seemed destined for the presidency, she had thought at the time. Although he was five years older than she was, Vonette was aware of Bill and made it a point to know everything that he did.

But that had been quite a few years ago. Now, she was at college herself. Her world had expanded greatly since those younger days growing up in a very small town.

Clutching the envelope in her hand, unsure of what to make of this note, Vonette decided to show it to her father when he came home for lunch that day.

Mr. Zachary arrived a few minutes before lunch was ready. Sifting through the mail on the small table in the foyer, he glanced up when his young daughter approached him. He smiled at her. Mr. Zachary was a hard-working man, who was well respected in the community. But she knew him as a man who most of all, loved his family. With her envelope in hand, Vonette slipped her arm through her father's and walked with him to the dining room.

Peering over the letter at the lunch table, he laughed, 'Oh, oh! Small town boy goes to Hollywood and makes good!' Mr. Zachary lifted his eyes to gaze at his daughter. Putting the letter down, he picked up his fork and knife again. Mr. Zachary knowingly commented, 'He is coming home for his bride.'

Later, Vonette lay on her bed thinking about her father's response. She didn't like the idea that Bill Bright was coming home for a bride. Determined, Vonette decided she just wouldn't write back.

Summer passed quickly enough and before she knew it, she had returned to Denton for college in the midst of her fall semester. One evening, Vonette and her roommate sat talking.

'Well,' Vonette said smiling, 'There is always that first crush you have, you know the one where he is older than you and is just wonderful!'

Vonette thought back to that spring night when a young Bill Bright stood before an auditorium packed with people and delivered his speech.

'Well?' her roommate queried, noticing Vonette's dreamy expression. 'You sure don't look like that crush has ended!'

Vonette blushed. 'Well, it was the strangest thing. I received a letter from him this summer.' She continued, sheepishly, 'He told me that he had seen a movie star ... and she reminded him of me,' she finished, now fully embarrassed.

'What!' her roommate exclaimed, sitting up on her bed. 'Tell me you wrote back!'

'Well, no, I didn't,' Vonette admitted, explaining her father's opinion on the subject. It didn't seem that bad now, she thought, as she sat and told her roommate of Bill Bright. It had been a sweet note, she thought, sadly.

'Well, there's no time like the present,' her roommate responded decidedly, picking up her robe to change for bed, 'You've got to write to him!'

So, Vonette decided to write to Bill. One page led to another, until she stuffed ten pages into an envelope. Once she had started writing, it just seemed to flow naturally. She wrote of university life. She wrote of all that had happened since they had last seen one another.

It wasn't long before Bill and Vonette were corresponding regularly, even talking on the telephone from time to time. They had many things in common. And it helped that they had known each other for fifteen years, and their families were close as well. She was a church-going girl, Bill knew. He would not be involved with anyone who did not have faith in Jesus Christ.

Bill had had an upcoming business trip across the southwest, visiting customers in Phoenix, Arizona; El Paso, Texas, and finally Dallas, which was one half-hour from Denton where Vonette was in school. He asked her if she would be available for a date when he came through Texas. She agreed, and he asked if he could accompany her to the Red Bud Ball. And now, here was Bill, on her doorstep.

Bill and Vonette had not seen each other in several years. But when Vonette appeared at the door, Bill was awestruck. Vonette was just as beautiful as any Hollywood movie star; he grinned as he closed her car door after her.

Both had been thinking about this first meeting quite a lot. As mile stretched into mile on Bill's trip east, he couldn't stop thinking about her. In fact, Bill was considering whether or not to ask Vonette to marry him on this, their first date. But was this from God? he wondered. As he drove, Bill prayed and asked God to lead him.

'In fact, Lord,' he prayed with inspiration, 'stop me from marrying her if this is not Your will.'

Finally, Bill realized that an inner peace had settled deep within him. It seemed that this was of God. He was to marry Vonette Zachary.

All of this was new to Bill. Never had he thought of marriage with any of the girls he had dated previously. And never before had he considered how moving God to top priority would change everything: even how he made decisions!

Vonette, as well, had done a lot of thinking. She realized before seeing Bill that if he was still the man she remembered, then she was in love with him. His letters and phone calls had only added to what Vonette knew to be true about Bill. This first meeting might clinch it for her.

At the ball, surrounded by hundreds of beautiful Texas State University women and their dates, Bill and Vonette spent some private time over dinner. Vonette, remembering Bill to always have a plan, asked him what he had in mind for his future.

'I have definite plans,' he replied, his eyes lowering, 'for my business, success, travel ... and marriage.' Raising his eyes to rest on Vonette's face, he said softly, 'But my plans depend on you.'

The band played softly behind the couple. Vonette took in Bill's meaning.

'Vonette, will you marry me?' Bill asked, leaning forward. Breaking the silence, he added, 'We'll ride horses in the Hollywood hills, travel to Europe – all over the world. You'll have the best of everything – a home in Bel Air, clothes, your own car.'

'Bill, ' Vonette said, softly, with eyes glistening, 'I... I am in love with you,' adding quickly, 'but, this is so sudden! Can we take a couple of days to think and talk about it?'

'Of course,' Bill nodded, 'Take the time you need.'

'But you should know,' he finished, standing up, and reaching for her hand to lead her to the dance floor, 'that my mind is made up. In fact, I am planning on visiting your parents when I go home.'

By Sunday, Vonette had made her decision. She would marry Bill Bright. That night, Vonette wrote a letter to her parents, telling them of her anticipated engagement.

Bill drove to Coweta. He looked down at the speedometer. Again, he was fifteen miles over the speed limit! Every time he thought of Vonette, his foot punched the gas pedal. He slowed the car back down again.

But as he thought of Vonette once more, how beautiful and smart she was, how she had her own goals, how she would fit into Hollywood, and how they shared so many childhood memories, the accelerator crept up once more.

When Bill arrived at the Zachary home, however, his enthusiasm was tempered. Vonette's letter had arrived before Bill did, and the surprise it carried had not worn off. Confused, Vonette's parents told Bill that they thought highly of him but had just no idea that Vonette and Bill had been dating. The last they knew, Vonette had decided not to write back to Bill that previous summer.

The Zacharys processed through their thoughts, finally approving of the relationship. Bill and Vonette could proceed with their engagement. However, they added, time was needed. They wanted Vonette to finish school. And, concerned over the quickness of everything, they told Bill that they wanted to give Vonette time to grow, to be certain that she knew what she was doing.

'Three more years,' Bill thought, disheartened, when he heard the Zacharys' decision. 'But it makes sense, and they obviously care about her.' Bill agreed to wait the three years until after Vonette had graduated from college.

'In the meantime, young man,' Mrs. Zachary volunteered, looking at her husband for his approval, 'I would be glad to chaperone Vonette for two weeks next summer to see you in California. It will give me an opportunity to see the life you have created for yourself,' Mrs. Zachary concluded, with a wink.

With three years ahead of him, Bill flung himself into work, ministry at the church, and seminary. Over that time, Bill and Vonette corresponded and talked on the telephone. Visits were infrequent, but they seemed to confirm their desire to spend the rest of their lives together.

However, another awareness was growing in Bill. And it was unsettling. As Bill began to grow as a Christian, he began to notice a difference between how he talked about Jesus and how Vonette discussed Jesus. The more he and Vonette talked and wrote, Bill began to suspect that what he had assumed to be a real faith in Vonette, was in fact church membership only.

Stress began to enter into their discussions. The more Bill pointed to certain Scripture verses, encouraging Vonette to read them, or shared events in his life as 'answers to prayer,' the further the divide seemed. Vonette had never heard of anything like what Bill was saying. She began to think he was a religious fanatic.

Bill's letters, once humorous, lively and romantic, now turned serious. When Bill told her that God would be first in their marriage, Vonette balked. She thought a man should put his family first, not God.

Dare to be Different

Bill's agony grew. He was growing in leaps and bounds in his faith, but Vonette seemed to be heading in the opposite direction. Vonette was approaching graduation. But instead of growing closer with greater anticipation of their impending wedding, they seemed to be drifting further apart. In fact, Vonette told Bill she wasn't sure about religion outside of church attendance. Nor, she expressed to him, did she see the Bible's relevancy to daily life.

Bill had returned to Hollywood and had already entered Fuller seminary. He regularly went out with his classmates, or with members of the church to talk to strangers about Christ. He wanted to tell Vonette that same good news. But the more he thought about how to explain it to her, the more he realized that he could not be the one to do it. He didn't want romance to enter into her decision.

Around that same time, Bill, together with his 'Burning Heart' brothers and Miss Mears, were planning a conference at the Forest Home. Hundreds of college students would be invited to come to listen to wonderful speakers.

'I've got it!' Bill thought excitedly. He would invite Vonette to come to the conference. Perhaps God would use these speakers, and the hundreds of winsome college students to show Vonette how attractive Christianity was. Growing more excited at the idea, Bill wrote and invited Vonette to come west to attend the conference with him. In his mind, this would be a final opportunity to resolve this issue. It was a step of faith. He knew he was committed to Christ. Through sadness, Bill knew that he couldn't marry Vonette – and nor did it seem that she would want to – if things didn't change.

A few days later, Bill's letter sat opened to the side of Vonette's lunch tray. She was in the dining hall with her closest friends, picking at her food. She knew the invitation was important to Bill, but she also sensed his agenda. With a growing sadness, Vonette knew that everything was coming to a decision point.

Barely touching her food, Vonette stood and picked up her tray. 'I'm either going to rescue him from this religious fanaticism,' she said sadly to her friends 'or, I'm going to come back without a ring.' Leaving the cafeteria, Vonette twisted the diamond ring on her left hand. It had held such promise three years ago, but now seemed to weigh heavily on her finger.

At the conference, Vonette met many of Bill's friends. They were exactly as Bill had described. They were warm and friendly, inviting and fun. And they certainly showed Vonette that Bill was not alone in his exuberance about God. But somehow that only seemed to confirm what she now knew she needed to do.

Taking a walk with Bill on the grounds of Forest Home, Vonette told him that the conference had indeed made it very clear to her that she did not believe in Christ the way he did. Meeting his friends had confirmed that.

'I don't want to stand in your way,' she told Bill, softly, stopping and turning to face him. With tears glistening, she told Bill that maybe the best thing to do was to break the engagement. She would go back home and take a teaching job. 'We should probably go our separate ways,' she broke off, with a choke.

Bill stared at the ground, heart heavy.

Slowly, he raised his own moist eyes to meet Vonette's. 'Would you do one thing for me?' he asked her, softly. 'Would you agree to talk to Miss Mears tonight after the session?'

Vonette felt skeptical. But, with the prospect of losing this dear man forever, she agreed to meet with Miss Mears, not sure how this one conversation could possibly change anything.

That evening, Miss Mears spoke of faith, of sin, of confession and the filling of the Holy Spirit. She then invited people to tell their own stories, to talk about what they were learning, or how God was dealing with them regarding sin. Four hours later, the meeting concluded.

Bill had already asked Miss Mears if she would agree to meet his fiancée who did not know Jesus personally. Miss Mears agreed and after the session, Vonette and Bill walked to her cabin. Bill remained outside, pacing and praying for the conversation. One hour passed. Then, two.

In the cabin, the two women quickly realized they shared much in common. Vonette had minored in chemistry in college and had just received her teaching credentials. Miss Mears told Vonette that she taught chemistry in Minnesota. Sensing an understanding heart, Vonette told Miss Mears about the afternoon's conversation with Bill. She admitted her realization at how different their faiths looked.

'Things should be practical and workable,' she told Miss Mears. 'With my mind for science, that is one of the reasons I question the validity of Christianity.'

The teacher assured Vonette that she understood these questions. Using language and illustrations from chemistry, Miss Mears explained to Vonette how someone could practically and personally know Christ.

Finally, Vonette asked if she, too, could meet Jesus Christ.

Quoting Revelation 3:20, Miss Mears encouraged Vonette, 'Jesus says, "Behold, I stand at the door and knock: if any man hear my voice, and open the door, I will come in to him, and will sup with him, and he with me.'" She went on to explain that to invite Christ into her life was a matter of turning her entire life over to Him.

Vonette thought for a moment. She had nothing to lose, and everything to gain, she realized. Bowing her head, Vonette prayed and asked Christ to come into her life.

Bill stopped pacing the moment he heard the cabin door open. Seeing Vonette's expression, he knew at once that something had changed. She ran into his arms, filled with great joy. Looking back at the cabin, Bill mouthed the words, 'Thank you,' to Miss Mears, who stood in the doorframe smiling. She nodded at Bill, but looked upward. It was God's doing, she seemed to say.

Over the next few days, Vonette began to realize that a change had occurred. Suddenly, when she prayed, it felt as if her prayers didn't stop at the ceiling any more. They went right on through. Love just seemed to flow from her, where effort had once existed.

Three months later, on December 30, Bill Bright and Vonette Zachary, surrounded by friends and family, entered the little Methodist Church in Coweta to be joined before God. This was more than just a ceremony. They both knew God personally, and they were inviting him to direct their lives as a couple.

The Contract

Bill and Vonette sat in the back of Hollywood Presbyterian Church. The Wednesday evening business meeting was well attended; more than a thousand people sat in the pews. Bill reached for Vonette's hand as they waited for the meeting to begin. Vonette turned and smiled at her handsome husband. The young couple still thought of themselves as newly married, even though two years had passed.

Vonette had been teaching at a school in Los Angeles. They were not in need of extra money but she wanted to put her university training to use. Bill agreed. He was proud of his wife and pleased with her sense of ambition.

In addition to their full-time jobs, they were both involved at Hollywood Presbyterian Church. Bill worked with the church's young people that now numbered several hundred. Weekly, he led 120 of the more dedicated young men and women to reach out to those in need. They visited prisons, hospitals, and street missions. And when he had a spare moment, Bill continued to work on finishing seminary.

The meeting came to order. Motions were called for and passed. The next order of business, it was announced, was the discussion regarding nominations for deacons. A list was read of candidates that had been selected.

Bill's head shot up. Had he heard correctly? Vonette looked over at her husband, with an expression of mingled pride and surprise. 'Did you know you were on the list?' she whispered.

'No,' Bill whispered back.

With the list read, the floor was opened for any opinions from the congregation. A man stood, and Bill looked over at him. It was a former business partner, a member of the family with whom he had had a financial dispute.

Surveying the congregation, the man cleared his throat. He then said he could not support the nomination of Bill Bright.

'He is dishonest,' he boldly asserted. Another family member stood next to him. 'I agree,' he spoke, nodding, 'He does not deserve the privilege or responsibility.' He sat down.

Shock washed over the room. Awkward silence remained. Bill, at first surprised to hear his name mentioned from the front, now sat speechless. He felt stunned and humiliated. If there was anything the Bright men could boast about, it was that they were known for their honest dealings. Now, before hundreds of church members – people who mattered to Bill more than he could imagine....

Slowly, the senior pastor, Dr. Louis Evans rose to his feet. He announced that the business meeting would recess for a moment. The nominating committee needed a moment to reconsider its recommendation. The committee members stood and moved to a room off the sanctuary. Murmuring began to hum throughout the large room, and voices grew louder. Bill leapt to his feet, and quickly flew through the back doors. Rounding the outside of the building, Bill spotted a door leading to the committee meeting.

Breathless, he entered the room. Dr. Evans stood before the group. 'Dr. Evans,' Bill panted, 'please take my name off the list. I wouldn't want to do anything that might hurt the credibility of the church....'

Dr. Evans raised a hand to restrain the wounded man from speaking further. He looked down at the committee before him.

'I am aware of the situation that has led these men to raise their objections to Bill Bright's nomination. I have been made aware of all of the issues, and have examined the situation carefully.' Dr. Evans paused, 'And I am of the opinion that Bill Bright has been falsely accused. Moreover,' Dr. Evans finished, 'I urge you to leave this man's name on the list of individuals nominated for the position of deacon.'

Bill stared at Dr. Evans. There had been no hesitation on his part, thought Bill. None. Never before had he experienced such a bold declaration of affirmation from anyone. 'He ... he trusts me,' Bill realized.

Bill left the room, stepping through the side door. He walked slowly around the building, wiping away tears. Quietly, he slipped into his seat next to Vonette. They sat in silence, for Bill did not know what to say.

Dr. Evans led the group back into the sanctuary. The meeting was called back from recess. The committee spokesman announced that they had considered the accusations brought against Bill Bright. In their opinion, he concluded, Bill Bright should remain on the list of recommended nominees for deacon.

Throughout the room, applause exploded. Before Bill knew what was happening, throughout the congregation, people began rising to their feet. The applause grew louder. Relief washed over Bill. He struggled to grasp what had just happened. He would not forget that moment.

Nor, however, would he forget the earlier moment of gut-wrenching agony when his pride had been sliced to bits. God was at work in Bill's life, and it was only the beginning.

Bill was appointed a deacon not long after that evening.

He began to visit the sick and the elderly, hoping to bring comfort. On more than one occasion, as Bill left the rooms of those he visited, he felt he had been more comforted than they had. From those visits, he learned that happiness was contentment no matter the circumstances. He also began to serve communion on Sundays. He learned great lessons from this responsibility as well. He had not understood the focus on the blood of Jesus, something that seemed so primitive and pagan. But after reading Hebrews 9:22, 'Without the shedding of blood is no remission [of sin],' Bill suddenly realized what the cross meant. As he served church members' communion, he began to weep with gratitude as he realized what the shedding of blood cost Christ because of Bill's sin.

Bill was learning a lot. But his involvement and responsibilities just continued to increase that next year. It would soon take its toll.

One Sunday morning, Bill and Vonette drove to church for worship and Bible study. Upon arriving, Bill was immediately pulled aside and told of a crisis counseling matter with a young woman in the college and career department. This young woman, unmarried, had become pregnant. To make matters worse, her father was a prominent evangelist. Bill hurried off to join two others for a spontaneous counseling session with the young woman. Vonette, meanwhile, upon turning around, suddenly did not know where Bill had gone. Shrugging, Vonette decided she would probably meet up with him in the study.

When Bill did not appear, Vonette walked alone to the church sanctuary for worship. Bill did not show up for the church service either. Vonette sat alone. Soon, even the worship service had ended and there was no sign of Bill. As the last person left the sanctuary and the lights were turned off, Vonette didn't know what to do but find their car. She walked slowly out to the parking lot.

Where was Bill, she asked over and over in her mind. She had waited for him before, but when it had grown really late, he had always sent a note. The questions and the annoyance grew. One hour passed. Anxious thoughts now accompanied frustration. The second hour passed. Worry and irritation each whispered in Vonette's ear. It was almost the third hour when Bill finally emerged from the building.

By now, Vonette was hot.

The ride home was long. 'What if the roles had been reversed?' Vonette asked Bill, fuming. 'What would you have expected from me?' As Bill listened to his wife express her displeasure, he began to realize how he was at fault. Having thought he was doing the right thing in focusing on this ministry situation, he was quickly made aware of how insensitive he had been to his wife. The discussion continued through their Sunday dinner and into the afternoon. Bill began to realize that this incident was only the tip of the iceberg. The longer they sat at the dining room table and talked, Bill began to think of their life from Vonette's perspective.

He had pulled her into his very busy life of business, ministry with college men and women, church activities, and seminary. Had he added a wife to his life like he added activities? Bill suddenly realized how insensitive he had been. Vonette was not an activity. She was his partner. She had not received the attention from him that she deserved. Here was this wonderful gift from God, he thought sorrowfully, yet, he had not treated her that way.

Bill asked Vonette what her expectations for marriage had been. After hearing from her, Bill told her of his own. Suddenly, Bill had an idea.

'I propose that we each take a piece of paper, and separately write down our expectations for marriage before God. Then, we'll come back together and ask God what He wants us to do with them.'

Vonette agreed. She went to the desk and pulled out two blank pieces of paper. She handed one to Bill. Vonette went into their bedroom and closed the door. Bill remained at the dining room table and began his list.

What do I want out of life? He wrote at the top of the page. As he thought over the question, he stroked his cheek with the pen. Bill often thought of things on a grand scale. This was no different.

He had come to California with a list of goals. He wanted to become a successful businessman. All of his ventures to that point – confections, oil and cattle – certainly suggested that he would do well. He had money in his pocket, sporty cars, a nice home, and a growing business. Politics had once been a goal, as had becoming a lawyer.

Things had changed drastically, Bill mused. He had not applied to law school, but seminary. He no longer spent as much time at the company but spent many hours at church. Ministry now replaced material wealth as a driving ambition. He now wanted to be expendable for Christ, he thought.

'But do I?' he suddenly asked himself. Straightening up, Bill wondered if the goals he had were his, and not Jesus Christ's.

Bill suddenly realized that being expendable for Christ meant that it needed to be on Christ's terms, not his. Bill's ideas, his goals, his pride and his priorities had all been tested that year. Would Bill be obedient? Today, his marriage was on the table. Would it be Christ's marriage, or his?

Bill put his pen to the paper.

I renounce every single thing to the control of the Lord Jesus Christ. I place my life, my marriage, my family, my home, my business, my ministry, seminary training – all that I own or ever will own – under the Lordship of Christ.

Bill thought of the apostle Paul's description of himself from Romans 1:1: 'Paul, a bond-servant of Christ Jesus, called as an apostle, set apart for the gospel of God. ...' That was it, thought Bill. To be a slave for Christ. That aptly described the obedient life that Bill desired to have before his Lord Jesus Christ.

In the next room, Vonette gazed out of the window. She, too, thought about what expectations she had had when she imagined life as Bill Bright's wife. What was it he had told her when he proposed that first night? she thought back. A home in Bel Air? Clothes and cars and travel to exotic places?

Vonette knew that her relationship with Christ in the last four years had changed many of her priorities. 'What are my fundamental goals for our marriage?' She asked herself. Then, she put pen to paper. Of a more practical mind than Bill, Vonette's list looked different.

Children; A home fit to entertain and minister to people from all walks of life; A car that was appropriate for their life of ministry.

Vonette thought for a moment more. Something was missing. There was something else. She thought for a moment. She wanted not only the outward appearance of a Christian marriage. She wanted her marriage to belong to Christ. After a few moments, she found the words to these feelings, writing one more item on her list: *God's blessing.*

Bill was reading in the living room when Vonette came

out of the bedroom. They took turns comparing their lists. At first, the lists seemed very different. But as Bill and Vonette talked, they realized that the real difference was how they looked at the world. Bill had big visions for life. Vonette saw the practical day-to-day side of life. Each had written a 'surrender' to God's plan in his or her own way.

Having originally thought they should combine their lists to create one 'mission' statement for their family, they quickly realized that the lists complemented each other perfectly and should be left alone.

'Let's leave these as they have been written,' Bill told Vonette, 'They are our "Contract with God."'

Vonette smiled at her husband. Bill took his pen and signed his name to what he had written. Vonette took the pen from Bill's hand and signed her name at the bottom of her list. Bill reached for his wife's hand, and sliding to his knees, invited her to join him in prayer together.

The young couple confessed their desire to surrender their entire lives to God's control. In faith, they invited God to do whatever He wanted to do through them, His slaves, for His glory. Whatever the cost, they were His bondservants. They were 'under contract.'

When they finally rose to sit back on the couch, the sun was sinking into the western horizon. After a day of turmoil and intense examination, peace settled upon the couple. They felt the release of complete surrender to God for their marriage and every activity and decision ahead. The future seemed clearer.

Little would the couple realize that in just twenty-four hours, God would give them an opportunity to put their new 'contract' into action.

Jumping in with Both Feet

Thump. Thump. Thump. Thump. Bill's feet pounded the pavement, keeping a steady rhythm. It was midnight and the moon's light brightened the path for him and his study partner. Bill's infectious enthusiasm had coaxed his friend to join him in keeping pace through the quiet neighbourhood streets. Bill's heart felt like it would burst. But it was not from the exercise. He had just had such a profound experience that words failed him. All he could think to do was go running.

One hour earlier, with Vonette asleep, Bill and his companion sat at the dining room table studying for a Hebrew exam the next day. Bill's Hebrew Bible was open to Psalm 8. They were working on verse 4:

כִּי־אֶרְאֶה שָׁמֶיךָ מַעֲשֵׂי אֶצְבְּעֹתֶיךָ יָרֵחַ וְכוֹכָבִים אֲשֶׁר כּוֹנָנְתָּה׃

Each man let the Hebrew words roll off his tongue.

'Kî|-'er'è šämÊkä ma'áSê 'ecBü`ötÊ°kä yareh wükôkäbîm 'ášher Kônäntâ,' they sounded out slowly. This was hard work, thought Bill. He looked at his English Bible to check his translation. *O Lord, our Lord, the majesty of your name fills the earth! Your glory is higher than the heavens. You have taught children and nursing infants to give you praise. They silence your enemies who were seeking revenge. When I look at the night sky and see the work of your fingers – the moon and the stars you have set in place. ...*

There it was, Psalm 8:4: ... *What are mortals that you should think of us, mere humans that you should care for us?*

Dare to be Different

'We are termites, mere termites in comparison to God,' thought Bill, reflecting upon the verse, 'and yet, he loves us and draws us to him. How wonderful! How amazing!'

It was just one day after Bill and Vonette had surrendered their lives and their marriage to God. Life had continued. Bill had gone to work that day, as had Vonette. And there was this Hebrew exam he needed to study for. But he knew he felt different. He was still basking in the moment he had with Vonette. He had surrendered everything in his life. He felt poised for whatever God would bring.

Suddenly, Bill sensed that the room had changed. It was unlike anything he had experienced. Immediately, he realized it could only be the presence of God. Bill put his Bible down. He closed his eyes, and prayed to God, 'Do you have something to say to me?'

The sense that God was there was so strong, that Bill knew all he could do was wait expectantly for whatever God wanted to say to him. Bill didn't hear a voice, or see a person or bright lights. But God was there. Bill just knew it. At the same time, Bill felt peace and excitement. He was enveloped in God's presence. He was aware of the holiness of God and of his own unworthiness. Yet, like Psalm 8:4, God had taken notice of him, a termite. And Bill felt drawn to God. Just as suddenly, Bill's mind was filled with purpose. He suddenly knew what God wanted him to do.

Bill once more became aware of the Hebrew Bible before him. His friend was still sitting beside him, unaware of Bill's experience. Bill was unable to speak. His heart was racing, and he was filled with unbounded energy. He had to do something. He would explode if he sat in that room for another minute. Turning to his friend, Bill had exclaimed, 'Let's go running!'

As he pulled on his shoes, Bill's mind raced with excitement. Could he have been prepared for this idea if he and Vonette had not placed their entire lives before God just twenty-four hours earlier? It was absolutely impossible to believe that God would have entrusted such a vision to Bill if he had not submitted everything to Jesus.

Bill ran until he no longer could. They ran back to the house. Calling an end to studying, Bill's friend packed up his books and went home to get some sleep before the exam the next day. Still trembling with excitement, Bill knew he wouldn't have been able to study anyway. But he also knew that he couldn't sleep. Bill went into the bedroom, and began to pace, tears streaming down his face. Vonette stirred, awakened by what sounded like feet shuffling and what she thought were sobs and ... was that laughter?

Seeing her stir, Bill went over to the bed and apologized for waking her. But unable to contain all that was inside, jumbled words began to spill from Bill's mouth. He tried his best to describe his overwhelming experience with God.

'It was a divine encounter with God, Vonette. I can't explain it, except to say that I was enveloped in God's presence. What was most on his heart was suddenly imparted to mine: to seek and save the lost,' Bill told her, excitedly.

'I saw us reaching the world with the good news of Jesus Christ ... of every person in the world having the opportunity to know Christ,' Bill paused at the thought, 'Can you imagine it, Vonette? Billions of people hearing the message of God's love and forgiveness through Christ?' Bill whispered, still awestruck at the idea. The magnitude of the proposition overwhelmed Bill.

'But I sensed it could and would be accomplished,' Bill continued, firm resolve sounding in his voice. 'God is going to use us to tell this generation about Jesus Christ. We are going to see the Great Commission fulfilled in this generation. And …' Bill paused for a moment, looking at his young wife, 'I think I am to start by reaching out to tomorrow's leaders on the college campus … It won't end there,' Bill quickly said, 'But it will begin there.'

The words were already forming in his mind: 'Reach the campus for Christ today – Reach the world for Christ tomorrow.'

'Do you remember how hard a time I had trying to find places for us to take our students to talk to people about Jesus Christ?' Bill asked Vonette, who was now sitting upright, her pillow behind her. She nodded. 'All of my calls to prisons and street missions brought the same news. They already had churches signed up to visit them. I remember thinking, "Surely there was a group in Los Angeles that needed to hear about Jesus Christ that had no church group flocking to it,"' Bill continued, pausing for a moment. 'And then there was the conversation I had with Billy.'

Vonette nodded again. Earlier in the year, Bill had met with the not-yet-famous evangelist Billy Graham. As they talked, Bill described his dilemma: his heart was moving away from the business and toward ministry. He was searching to know what to do with his life.

'Well, what motivates you?' Billy Graham asked Bill, thoughtfully.

Bill wondered for a moment. What did get him excited? Immediately, he thought of the young adult group at Hollywood Presbyterian Church.

'Students,' Bill replied, without hesitation.

'Well, if students are what motivate you, perhaps you should give your life to students,' Billy had told him.

'It all fits, doesn't it?' Bill whispered, once again overwhelmed that God would give him, a termite in God's kingdom, such a job.

Vonette smiled at her husband, and leaned forward to hug him. Initially, when she had woken up, she thought for a second that maybe her husband had gone crazy because of too much studying. But as she listened, she agreed that God had indeed met with Bill. She loved his passion to tell people about Christ. She, too, was overwhelmed by the events of the past two days. Yesterday, God had made it clear they were to be obedient. Now, God was giving them a big and bold plan. It was far more than they had anticipated.

The next day, Bill's exam passed by in a blur, after which he walked across the seminary grounds to his car. Suddenly, he remembered his mentor, Dr. Wilbur Smith. 'I must tell him,' thought Bill. Hurrying across campus, Bill found the professor in his office. Excitedly, Bill told him of his experience and vision. Dr. Smith began to pace his office. 'Indeed,' he muttered, 'This is of God…this is of God…'

He turned to Bill, who was thrilled that this godly man would also be excited. Dr. Smith told Bill he would think and pray about it all.

The next morning, as Bill sat in class, someone rapped on the door. As Bill looked up at the door, he was surprised to see it was Dr. Smith. More surprising was the sight of Dr. Smith motioning for Bill to step out to join him in the hall. His professor's interruption and exuberance caught Bill off-guard. He hurried out into the hallway. Dr. Smith handed him a note. The letters *CCC* were written across the page. Puzzled, Bill looked up at Dr. Smith.

Pointing his finger excitedly at the scrape of paper, Dr. Smith motioned that Bill read further. Below the three letters were written the words: *Campus Crusade for Christ*. With a twinkle in his eye, Dr. Smith told Bill, 'I believe God has given me the name for your vision.'

After a brief prayer, the two men parted. Bill slipped back into class, anxious for the bell to ring. He could not wait to rush home and tell Vonette of today's exciting development.

As Bill and Vonette prayed together in the evening, she became more and more excited. Questions came quickly. How do we start this and where? With whom? When?

Bill and Vonette immediately realized that they had to start with prayer. Nothing should happen that they had not prayed for first. They set up a twenty-four-hour prayer chain of fifteen-minute intervals each. They invited friends from seminary and Hollywood Presbyterian to pray with them. No plans were made that were not committed to prayer. Any answer from God would come through prayer.

Bill now knew what God wanted him to do with his life. He realized he had to start right away. Immediately. Vonette agreed. They should jump into full-time ministry right away. There was no turning back. There was no reason to delay. 'I cannot imagine pursuing anything else,' thought Bill. Weighing up his many responsibilities, Bill evaluated what should stay and what should go.

Bill pondered his seminary degree. No seminary degree would change what he knew he was going to do for the rest of his life. It was time to leave seminary, even though he had nearly finished all of his coursework. Vonette was not so easily convinced. 'All that work,' she pointed out. But Bill was determined. It later became clear that the title of 'layman' rather than 'clergyman' would open far more doors to tell strangers about Jesus Christ.

Bill described the vision of Campus Crusade for Christ with friends and colleagues, and asked for their counsel. He was encouraged each time. They voiced their support. As he continued to pray for God's guidance, Bill realized he needed wise men and women who were committed to Christ to oversee this new fledgling ministry. Bill found them and asked them to serve on Campus Crusade for Christ's board. He went first to his advisor, and the one who had named the organization, Dr. Wilbur Smith. Next, he asked Henrietta Mears, who was an important influence in Bill and Vonette's lives.

The third person Bill asked was Billy Graham and, finally, Richard Halverson, one of Bill's 'Burning Heart' brothers. Several more men and women in ministry, in business or from the seminary were also invited to join the board.

Bill now knew exactly where to begin. Student leaders today would be the future's leadership. To reach the world with the good news of Jesus Christ, he would meet first with the college influencers. And where were the campus' social and intellectual leaders? In sororities[1] and fraternities, Bill realized.

Their first target was the Kappa Alpha Theta sorority house on the campus of the University of California of Los Angeles (UCLA). Prior to that first meeting, Bill prayed. He sensed that this was not merely a test of the immediate present, but the whole vision of Campus Crusade for Christ was on the line. Bill prayed and asked God to confirm the vision by bringing one person forward to respond positively to the message that evening.

The sorority women gathered in the living room. One by one, three of the young men and women from Hollywood Presbyterian got up and told the women about knowing

[1] Sororities - social clubs for female students.

Jesus Christ personally. Bill then got up and told the group about the person of Jesus. He told the gathered group they could know God personally because of what Jesus did on the cross. As Bill finished, he invited the women to consider inviting Jesus Christ into their hearts. Then, Bill made a specific plea to the women individually. If any woman wanted to invite Christ into her heart, she could get up and tell him personally at that moment.

Bill dropped his head and his eyes, allowing time for the women to consider the invitation. He heard a woman approaching him. He raised his head.

He was stunned. A line had formed behind this one young woman in the center of the room. Of the sixty women who had attended the meeting, half now stood in line. God had heard his prayer.

As the meeting concluded, Bill stood to make an announcement.

'Tomorrow night, we will have another meeting in our home,' Bill told the women, gesturing to include Vonette. 'I invite you to bring your friends. Please come!' he smiled. 'We would love for you to join us tomorrow night.'

The following night, many did come, including several athletes, the editor of the school newspaper and musicians. Over the next few months, meetings took place all over the UCLA campus – in sororities, fraternities, dorm rooms, and locker rooms. More than 250 students committed their lives to Christ – including the student newspaper's editor, the top athletes, and the student body president. Soon, over the noon hour, the chimes for the campus could be heard playing out Christian hymns.

Campus Crusade for Christ had begun.

Making it Simple

A young man knelt by his bed with the two men. He asked Christ to forgive his sins and make him God's man. With tears glistening in his closed eyes, Bill Bright patted the young man's shoulder and nodded his agreement in prayer.

Bill left the UCLA dormitory. With him was his most recent recruit, his newest Campus Crusade for Christ staff member. He was in training with Bill. Turning, Bill asked him if they could pray for the young man for a moment. And so, stopping near a bicycle rack on the edge of the campus, the two men prayed briefly. Bill thanked God for a wonderful 'divine appointment.'

When they finished and began to walk toward the street, the young staff member asked Bill to explain something. 'Why did you call it a 'divine appointment?' he asked.

'Any opportunity to tell someone about Jesus is a "divine appointment" or God's doing,' Bill told the young man. 'I am responsible to do my part. Starting the conversation about Jesus Christ is man's responsibility. For example, when someone calls me and they realize they have dialed the wrong number, I see that as a divine appointment. I tell them that they haven't misdialed at all. In fact, I have something wonderful to share with them,' Bill told him, 'I take the opportunity to tell them the good news of Jesus Christ.'

'But,' Bill quickly interjected, reaching the spot where his car was parked, 'It is essential to remember that the results belong to God alone.' The young man nodded as Bill continued. 'Success in telling people about Christ is simply taking the initiative, in the power of the Holy Spirit, and leaving the results to God.'

Meanwhile, news of Campus Crusade for Christ's early ministry success at UCLA was spreading like wildfire. Bill and Vonette were spending more and more time talking about how to grow the new ministry.

Bill hung up the phone and walked to the kitchen where Vonette sat at the table, deep in paper. She looked up as he approached.

'Another pastor calling to ask if we can send a staff person to his local campus,' Bill told her, 'This time, it was a pastor from Arizona.' Bill could not help but smile at his wife. The vision was taking off.

Pastors in California had started the phone calls. Lately, the calls were coming from nearby states. Bill and Vonette had been considering whom they would invite to join them as staff members to meet the growing need.

'They've got to be college graduates,' Vonette said one day, 'Because, initially at least, we hope to reach college students.'

But the question Bill was grappling with was whether or not staff members needed to be seminary-educated. After an unsuccessful recruiting trip on seminary campuses, Bill sensed that God was not looking to build Campus Crusade for Christ with seminary graduates alone.

They were also talking about the goals of the ministry. It needed to be simple, and stay on target. Bill talked to staff members, board members, and Vonette. They were to reach the world with the gospel of Jesus Christ. They would win people to Christ. The first goal seemed obvious. *Win*, Bill had written down.

But they also wanted to train and equip new believers. Too many Christians told Bill stories of going home after conferences where they had made commitments to Christ, only to lose their way. Many did not know what to do to grow as believers. *Build,* Bill had written down.

Finally, Bill knew he didn't want new believers to become stagnant. 'Christianity is an adventure after all!' he'd exclaim. Communicating the gospel of Jesus Christ to others was not humdrum but some were too intimidated to tell people about Jesus. Bill understood that and realised that many people had just not learned how to start a conversation. There were too many wonderful Christians who had never learned how to communicate the truths about God's love through Jesus Christ to others. His own mother was an example. 'But Jesus has shown us what to do,' Bill would remind himself. 'He sent his own disciples out on their own to spread the message of God's salvation.' *Send,* Bill wrote down.

Win. Build. Send. Bill smiled at the simplicity of the strategy. It would be something people could easily remember. But something else was bothering Bill. He was becoming more convinced that they needed simpler ways to communicate the how-tos of Christianity. Churches around the nation were beginning to ask Bill to train their congregations to tell others about the good news of Jesus Christ. He wanted to help and one question kept rattling around in his head. 'How can we make the amazing truths of Scripture understandable to men and women in everyday language? Something that they can then take and give to their friends?'

Bill and Vonette's kitchen table had been the center of much publishing and editing work. They were continually editing materials they were using to tell college students about Jesus Christ. But they weren't there yet, thought Bill.

It was at a staff retreat that the issue reached a turning point. Bill had invited a Christian friend, who was a successful sales consultant to come and speak to his sixty assembled staff members.

'You need to have a clearly stated message. The more plainly and frequently stated, the better,' the consultant put forth, 'A common danger is to change your message. You become ineffective then. What you need is a pitch,' he stated simply. He pointed out several Christian leaders, each of whom had his or her own distinctive spiritual 'pitch.' They said the same thing, over and over.

'Take Bill Bright, for example,' he continued, 'He works with college students, but he also talks to executives, and prison inmates. Now, I'll tell you something … he thinks he has an unique message for each group, but do you know what? He doesn't! I would be willing to bet that he has one pitch. He tells every person the same thing.'

Bill recoiled in his seat. How dare he suggest that Bill used Madison Avenue marketing techniques to do God's work.

That afternoon, Bill went to a quiet place alone. He felt offended and resented the suggestion that he might not be led by the Spirit to tell people about Christ. He also realized, his ego had been taken down a notch. Bill knelt in prayer. He asked God to show him if there was any truth in the situation. Was there anything the Lord wanted to show him?

He began to write out what he commonly told people. He decided to write a first page with an executive in mind. He would write another page afterward, picturing a person on skid row. He began.

First, he wrote of God's love. *For God so loved the world that He gave His only begotten Son, that whosoever believes in him should not perish, but have eternal life (John 3:16).*

He, then, wrote of a plan that God had for a wonderful life. *[Christ says] 'I came that they might have life and have it abundantly' (John 10:10).*

Next, he showed that individuals are dead in their sins and without hope. Man is essentially separated from God. *All have sinned and fall short of the glory of God (Romans 3:23). The wages of sin is death (Romans 6:23).*

Third, Bill wrote, God has made provision for man's sin through His Son, Jesus Christ, who died on a cross for men's sins. He died in man's place. *God demonstrates his own love toward us, in that while we were yet sinners, Christ died for us (Romans 5:8).*

But Christ did not stay there, but rose again from the dead. *Christ died for our sins...He was buried...He was raised on the third day according to the Scriptures...He appeared to [Peter], then to the twelve. After that He appeared to more than five hundred... (I Corinthians 15:3-6).*

Jesus is, Bill continued to write, the only way to God. *Jesus said to him 'I am the way, the truth, and the life; no one comes to the Father but through me' (John 14:6).*

Finally, it was not enough to know those three points, but each person must individually receive Jesus Christ as his Savior and Lord. *But as many as received Him, to them He gave the right to become children of God, even to those who believe in his name (John 1:12).*

We receive Christ by faith, but that, too, is a gift, wrote Bill. *By grace you have been saved through faith; and that not of yourselves, it is the gift of God; not as a result of works, that no one should boast (Ephesians 2:8-9).*

We receive Christ by personal invitation, he pointed out, which means turning from oneself to God. That means trusting Christ to enter your life, forgive the sin and make you the person he wants you to be. *[Christ says] 'Behold, I stand at the door and know; if anyone hears My voice and opens the door, I will come in to him' (Revelation 3:20).*

Bill finished the first page. He sat for a moment, mentally shifting gears to begin to think about how he would talk to someone who lived on the streets. He began to write again. After several minutes, Bill put the pen down.

He put the pages side-by-side and blinked. They were almost exactly the same. The consultant was right, Bill realized. He had been explaining the same basic message with everyone. Well, Bill thought, if that was the case, then it should be made as clear as possible. And we should tell that one message often.

Bill wrote out what he called, 'God's Plan for Your Life' that included four points. Later that afternoon, Bill showed the finished product to his staff members. He then asked them to memorize it and use it when they told people about Christ. In future months, as his staff used 'God's Plan,' it became obvious that it was effective. It was a clear presentation of the main points of the gospel message, and more people were responding to it. It was revolutionary.

But Bill continued to revise it.

One evening, he sat hunched over the kitchen table. He was editing 'God's Plan' again. It has got to be relevant, Bill thought. So what was relevant to this generation? he asked himself.

The Cold War with the Soviet Union dominated almost everything they did, Bill thought. Beating the Russians was everyone's goal. Politicians campaigned on the issue. Movies were being made about it. It was a hot topic on the booksellers' lists. Since space was the next thing to conquer, the race to get to space before the Russians was foremost in people's thoughts. Scientists were in the news regularly. Scientific terminology flowed in regular conversation now.

'Hmmm,' Bill mused, out loud, 'How to take that and introduce God's plan to this generation?' Suddenly, a thought occurred to Bill, 'Physicists often talk about the physical laws that govern the physical universe,' Bill grew excited, 'Why not … yes, that's it!' Bill began to scribble. *Just as there are physical laws that govern the physical universe, so there are spiritual laws that govern our relationship with God.* He would call the booklet, *The Four Spiritual Laws*.

Now, Bill thought with new energy, how to put the rest of the booklet together? There was one important issue that bothered Bill. The order of the first two points. Do you begin with talking about man's sin, Bill questioned, or God's love?

Bill had done what most Christians did: they talked first of man's sin, because all men were sinful. But it bothered Bill. Everyone knew they were sinful, so why begin with a negative note? What about starting by saying, God loves you?

Bill realized it raised questions. Could you say that God loved all men? Was God's love the most important spiritual law of the universe? Bill thought deeply about his own experience and his theological training. To begin by saying that God loved you was more consistent with his own life. He had been drawn by the love of God. God's love had compelled him to do God's work. God's love in his life had made him aware that he was a sinner. The love of God had revealed his heart for what it was: self-centered, status-seeking, and money-loving.

'I was a happy pagan,' Bill thought. His heart was sinful – but as Bill studied God's word he came across countless stories which also told him that God loved even when people were unfaithful. And the apostle Paul reminded the Roman Christians that nothing could separate them from the love of God.

Yes, he had to start with the message of God's love. It would be closely followed by the truth of man's sinful condition, but it would start with God's love.

Bill ran downstairs to tell Vonette and the others. The reaction was mixed. Many were hesitant to approach the gospel in this way. Bill listened as they shared their responses. In the end, Bill knew that the greatest news – indeed the *good news* – he could offer to people was that God loved them *and* had a plan for their lives. It was true in his life. He knew it would be true in others' lives as well.

God Meeting Needs

Bill looked down at the financial figures. They told him how much money was needed to keep Campus Crusade for Christ going. Bill glanced at the map of the United States on the wall. Thumbtacks dotted the map, pointing to spots where campus ministries had sprung up. A map of the world had been purchased to keep this one company. There were staff members in South Korea, in Pakistan, and the Middle East. Soon, there would be a representative in Mexico.

It had now been twelve years since they had started. Campus Crusade had more than 154 staff, serving on forty-five campuses. Bill was also on the radio weekly in California.

Keeping a ministry afloat took a lot of money, Bill thought. His list was long: the conference center, rent; travel expenses; printing ministry materials. The sheer number of staff members was overwhelming. They were bursting at the seams and they needed more money to pay salaries.

Slipping to his knees, Bill began to praise God. He knew that God was providing for every need. He thanked God for the many ways he had taken care of them. He asked God again to provide the money that they needed and prayed that he would provide a place suitable to train new staff.

Rising to sit once more, Bill leaned back in his chair.

Memories came flooding back of how faithful God had been. He had provided money and had looked after them emotionally and spiritually. Bill often thought of the contract he and Vonette had signed ten years ago. In it, Bill had renounced materialism, or dependence on money. They depended on God for everything they needed.

In the beginning of the ministry, Bill had provided his new staff recruits with room and board, and $100 a month. His business had paid for all ministry expenses. But he soon realized that the ministry needs were getting so big that the business could no longer cope with it.

Bill had thought that his business skills would allow him to make enough money to take care of things. But he found himself spending more time working on money issues, rather than the actual ministry. Did God have other plans? Bill prayed about the dilemma for many months and discussed the issue with Vonette.

As Bill prayed, he thought back to the values with which he had grown up. Two stood out: first, the community took care of one another. Neighbors looked after each other. They shared their resources. His father, in particular, had taught him that. He shared what he had – even his new combine. When needs arose, Bill recalled, everyone pitched in to help.

The second value also ingrained in Bill was that no one person was better than another. There was mutual respect. His own father, although he had more resources than many other men in the community, respected his neighbors and worked alongside them when a need arose.

A plan began to form in Bill's mind. He approached the board with a suggestion. It would be revolutionary.

'I propose,' Bill began, 'that we ask each individual staff member to raise his or her own financial support for the ministry. Many of them, because they are on the front lines of ministry, have already formed teams of prayer supporters from their home churches, friends and family. They already sense that this needs to be a ministry in partnership with others. I also know that many of them are writing to their prayer teams reporting on ministry activity.

'I would ask the board and leadership of Campus Crusade to set the salary expectations.' Thoughtfully, he added, 'Our staff members have different situations – some are single, some are married, and others have children. With that in mind, I also recommend that there should be some flexibility to raise funds according to need.

'What I hope we will see is Campus Crusade for Christ being supported by the community where everyone pitches in to meet the needs.'

Bill turned and looked at Vonette. She smiled. He turned to survey the board.

'There is no one person better than another. Vonette and I signed a contract with the Lord that renounced any materialism on our part. With that in mind, Vonette and I will also raise our support like everyone else. We will submit to the salary requirement that you see as fair. Vonette and I will be paid the same as any other married staff couple.'

The board approved Bill's radical fund-raising plan. From that point on, anyone who became a staff member went through support-raising training. Before reporting to their new assignments, they had to have details of how they would raise their expenses from a team of people they knew.

As Bill had hoped, the decision to ask staff members to raise their salaries bonded them together. Everyone was depending upon the Lord to provide for needs.

Older staff helped younger staff. Everyone was dependent on God to provide for their income. As the organization grew and people were given positions of responsibility everyone knew that Bill and Vonette were just the same as any other married couple without children.

***

A knock sounded on the door of Bill's office. His assistant poked his head into the office and reminded Bill that his lunch appointment with a local businessman was minutes away. Bill thanked his assistant and turned back to the papers on his desk. Just then he caught sight of the picture of his family and he smiled.

God had provided a family for Bill and Vonette, a wonderful family, Bill thought. Here, too, God had his own plans.

During the first few years of their marriage, Bill and Vonette had learned they could not have children. It was sad news. Through tears, they asked God why? Their minds searched to understand: was God punishing them? Was He teaching them? What should they do with their hopes? Should they abandon all hope for a family and pour their lives into the ministry? Or should they try medical procedures or adoption?

They had given their lives over to God. With sad hearts, they gave this problem to God as well. Eventually, they were able to thank God that he knew best. Though they still did not understand, they accepted their circumstances and God's leading. They were *slaves of Jesus*.

They prayed that God might fill this empty place in their lives. And He did. Bill looked at his oldest son in the photo. *Zachary*. Almost six years after they were married, God provided Zachary through adoption. Shifting his gaze, Bill looked at the fourth figure in the photo. Four years later, God had brought Brad into their lives as well.

Vonette had her hands full with the three men in her life. She pulled back from her many activities as a staff member to focus on her family. Vonette wanted to be a good mother to her boys, and to support Bill with his responsibilities as leader of a growing ministry.

As Bill's travel increased, so, too, did the couple's commitment to supporting one another. Vonette prayed with the boys for their father on his trips. She pulled out maps, and they learned about the countries to which he had traveled. Bill called Vonette each day, wrote postcards and brought home gifts for the boys. When he was home, he made himself available to Vonette and the boys no matter what. Bill also made sure his sons met the Christian men and women he was meeting, and that they came to his meetings. And they had fun. Bill played ball or rode dune buggies with his sons ... and they hiked in the San Bernardino foothills.

Ah, those hills, Bill thought . What a miracle. He smiled, as he gathered his papers for the meeting. God was providing an extravagant place for them in the California hills.

Seven years earlier, a five-acre retreat center in Minnesota had been donated to Campus Crusade for Christ. It was a welcome gift, a place suitable to train their sixty staff members. They built a chapel and met for training. But it was not long before their numbers were overwhelming the little center. Now, the site was too small to take care of all of their needs. They needed to build a larger place in Minnesota, or look elsewhere. They began to pray about it.

Bill had received a phone call from his friend, George Rowan, a Los Angeles businessman. 'Do you know what just went up for sale?' he told Bill, excitedly. George continued, 'The Arrowhead Springs Hotel and Spa in the San Bernardino mountains!' George surged forward. 'And the best part is it is for sale at "a greatly reduced price!" You've got to go to look at it!'

Dare to be Different

Bill sent his assistant, Gordon Klenck, to check it over. Though he was known for approaching things conservatively, Gordon encouraged Bill to pursue the purchase. 'It would revolutionize the ministry,' he told Bill.

Bill agreed to view the famous hotel. He wondered, however, about the 'greatly reduced price'. It must have deteriorated drastically in the last twenty years.

Legend had it that Indian tribes brought their sick and wounded to its mineral hot springs. They called it 'Holy Land' and set aside their weapons at this place. They believed it brought healing. Then, in 1854, the first hotel and spa had been built there. In 1939, the current hotel had been built, financed by a group of film stars.

The biggest names in Hollywood had enjoyed the hotel and spa. Even Judy Garland from 'The Wizard of Oz' had been there for the opening gala. But when traveling by plane became easier, Las Vegas with its casinos and the beauty of Palm Springs grew. Fewer and fewer stars went to the San Bernardino mountains. It was slowly forgotten.

Bill got out of George's car. The road had wound through the hills above the city of San Bernardino. The remoteness of the place immediately appealed to Bill. Its splendor made his jaw drop.

The caretaker offered to take them on a tour. The men nodded absently, each mind calculating the size of the place against the size of the ministry. Would it work?

Arrowhead Springs had 1,800 acres. The hotel had 136 rooms, built for executives. There were ten private bungalows on the property, and dormitory facilities built for several hundred people. The men were shown an auditorium that could seat 700 people, a recreation building, four tennis courts, a stable and two swimming-pools.

Bill was surprised at how well the hotel had been maintained. It was fully furnished. Tables and chairs clustered in the bar. Beds were made, and extra linens were in the closets. Kitchen equipment, silverware, china – it was all there. All they would have to do was move in.

George whispered to Bill that the property was valued at $6.7 million. 'But,' he continued, 'the seller's firm asking price was $2 million. It's a good deal, Bill'. George finished whispering, as the men walked out through the large glass sliding doors that opened to the terrace.

Bill asked for a moment alone. He needed to pray. He moved back inside the hotel, as George and the caretaker moved further down the terrace. He walked past the reception desk, knelt beside a chair and, overwhelmed at all he had seen, bowed his head and began to pray.

'We've been praying for the very best place, Lord, and have asked you to direct us to a new facility. And I know that you are faithful to do that. If this is it, how will we raise $2 million? That seems impossible. Yet, I sense that you have led me here. How can I know for sure?'

Immediately, Bill felt as though God was speaking directly to his heart. He sensed God had been saving the property just for Campus Crusade for Christ.

'Okay,' Bill whispered, tears now glistening in his eyes, 'I don't know how you intend to provide for this, but I know you are able. Thank you for this gift. I claim this property in your name and for your glory.'

As Bill drove down the mountain, he was convinced that Campus Crusade for Christ would one day occupy the beautiful spot. He was so convinced that he half expected a phone call later that afternoon from someone offering him $2 million to purchase it.

The more he thought about it, the more he was convinced that God already had a plan in place that would provide the $2 million. He thought of the time when he had been in his office on a Saturday morning, on his knees, praying for an urgent need of $485. In prayer, Bill was startled to hear a knock on the door. It was the postman, carrying a registered letter. Bill needed to sign for it.

As he opened the envelope, a bank note fluttered to the floor. He quickly read the letter. It was from a family in Switzerland who had become Christians through Bill's ministry. They were writing to thank him. They wanted to express their appreciation. He picked up the bank note. It was for $500! The $485 need had been miraculously met.

As Bill thought about Arrowhead Springs, he believed they should not write letters inviting people to invest in the property. Rather, the staff members prayed. For fourteen months, they prayed that if God wanted them to have Arrowhead Springs, he would provide the money. Bill and Vonette often knelt and asked God to work miraculously through their lives and that of Campus Crusade for Christ. They wanted God to receive all of the glory.

Meanwhile, as they waited in prayer, they were busy studying the property and figuring out what it would cost to run and operate. Bill told a few friends about the property. Some thought he was foolhardy. Others offered help. Bill made an offer of a $15,000 deposit and a $130,000 down payment, due within thirty days after signing the contract.

Bill shook with excitement when he received the call back. The offer had been accepted! 'With an empty checkbook, we are buying a $2 million property!' Bill told a friend, 'It has to be the greatest act of faith I have ever had a part in!'

The $15,000 had to be borrowed. Campus Crusade for Christ didn't have the $130,000 for the down payment either. At the last minute, friends of the ministry called to donate the initial money.

On December 1, 1962, Campus Crusade for Christ International moved its headquarters to Arrowhead Springs.

Setbacks and challenges seemed to shadow Bill as they raised the money. Businessmen offered to help, if Campus Crusade for Christ could raise certain amounts of money on its own. There were problems, several, but eventually, Bill and Vonette saw Arrowhead Springs paid for.

Bill was encouraged by God's word. Romans 8:28 reminded him that 'In all things God works for the good of those who love Him and have been called according to His purpose.' Hebrews 11:6 reminded Bill 'Without faith, it is impossible to please Him.' Galatians 3:11 encouraged him that 'The righteous shall live by faith.'

'You know the biggest lesson in all of this,' Bill told Vonette one night, after a particularly discouraging day. 'Today, I realized I did not know a better way to show that I trusted God than to say "Thank you". Just like it says in I Thessalonians 5:18, "Give thanks in all circumstances, for this is God's will for you in Christ Jesus."'

And so, that day, Bill had again gone to his knees in prayer. Not necessarily understanding God's purpose in a particularly bruising setback, by faith, Bill thanked God. He thanked him that in his wisdom and love, God knew a better way than Bill did. Bill was learning to take God at his word. After all, God was trustworthy.

Big God, Big Faith

Bill stood before sixty staff members from Asia and the Pacific Islands, dressed simply in a white guayabera[1] shirt. He began with prayer, his voice suddenly tender as he acknowledged his dependence upon God.

He and Vonette had arrived in Sydney, Australia, the day before. Bill had addressed several hundred men and women that evening. But now, as he finished his quiet prayer, he stood before staff members, many of whom he knew had suffered deeply for the gospel. Some had been beaten. Others were arrested and imprisoned. Still more had been deported from their homelands. He wanted to encourage them to press on, to strengthen their faith. This was family time. No pomp or circumstance.

It was thirty years since the day they had moved onto the Arrowhead Springs property. The years had added wrinkles and pounds, but he could still run circles around his many assistants.

'Someone once asked me,' he began, 'what one thing I would want to teach a new believer. It was a great question,' he acknowledged. 'I realized I would want a new believer to know the attributes of God. Why do we want to teach people that our God is great? That he is mighty? That he is holy, sovereign, and all-powerful? That he is loving and wise?' He looked deeply into the eyes of the men and women around the circle, 'Because the Christian life is a walk of faith.'

Bill continued, 'But faith must have an object. If you or

---

[1] A lightweight shirt/jacket popular in Latin America

I are ever to become anything other than spiritual weaklings, we must understand who God is. When we see God in a right way we are more likely to reach out to the world with the message of Christ.'

Bill paused for a moment. Dependence on God was crucial for these staff members who had gone through so much. He thought about how over the last thirty years God had taught him just that. Bill had learned to rely on the Holy Spirit to work through him. You had to rely on God in everything, Bill realized.

As he looked out at the weary faces listening to him his mind flashed back to the year 1967 when several of Bill's directors asked to meet with him. They had concerns. Pulling out a typed list, they read out their issues. Bill's leadership style was in question. He did not consult them when he made decisions. Others pointed out that he had focused too much on the college campus, and not enough on the rest of the world. People had expected that the world would be reached and Bill's own abilities as a preacher, and teacher were criticized. Theological differences were discussed too. Bill focused too much on repentance, others suggested.

As the list was put away, one of the men told Bill that they had come to the conclusion that Bill needed to step down from his position. He needed to resign, and allow more qualified men to fill the position of president.

Bill listened and remained calm, praying the whole time. But his heart ached, as he had loved these men fiercely and had handed over many areas of the ministry to them to manage. He had recruited them. He had trained them personally. But God gave Bill a right attitude at that moment and he did not react. Instead he took a deep breath, and said quietly, 'Let's talk about the concerns.'

'I am sorry that I've disappointed you,' he continued, 'Everyone has blind spots, and I certainly do, although I'm not convinced I am "that blind." But there is one thing you need to know,' he said gently but firmly. 'This organization began with two people and a vision from the Lord. At the end of the day, it may just be Vonette and me, but we started Campus Crusade for Christ, and we will continue to direct it. I will not step down. God gave me this vision and I am going to remain faithful to it.'

The meeting ended. Some of the leaders had hinted that if Bill remained in leadership, there would be a mass exit of staff. Bill wasn't sure what would happen to the organization.

As the door closed, Bill slid to his knees. He began to cry. A deep sense of betrayal cut through him. He poured his heart out to God. As he prayed, Bill realized that all he could do was leave it with the Lord. And he did. An hour later, Bill had moved on to other tasks. Bill knew this was God's ministry. He would watch over it. Over the next few days, Bill sought counsel. He talked to Vonette and respected ministry leaders. He even talked to the board of Campus Crusade for Christ. Were there things Bill had done that were wrong? Loving support and honest answers flowed from those with whom Bill talked. And, as he heard honest responses, he dealt with specific issues and asked forgiveness. Bill realized he was learning to love by faith – loving even those who criticized him.

Six leaders left Campus Crusade for Christ. But next summer, the largest number of new staff recruits ever arrived for training – more than 600 people from all over the world. God was still at work in Campus Crusade for Christ. Through the highs and the lows, Bill learned that the way through situations was dependence on God, who did not change. God was always holy, always in control. He knew everything, he was love, he was all-powerful.

In 1953, only two years after Campus Crusade for Christ was founded, Bill had decided he wanted to express his faith that they would reach the world for Christ in his generation. In a bold move, he began to sign his letters, *Yours for Fulfilling the Great Commission in This Generation.*

Bill knew that God would do it. What he had to do was to work at being faithful and trusting in God.

Turning again to the present and the sixty staff members before him, Bill concluded his message, with this encouragement: 'There is nothing too big for any of us to attempt for the glory of God. If our hearts and motives are pure, if what we do is according to the Word of God, he hears and is able to do more than we ask or even think.'

That afternoon Bill and Vonette boarded a plane to visit other international staff members. Bill began thinking about the many ways God had been working to reach this generation. He had been working in ways that hadn't been asked for or imagined. Bill fastened his seatbelt and leaned back in his seat. There were memorable moments. The campus at Berkeley, California came to mind.

They had called it the 'Berkeley Blitz.' Marxist professors and student riots characterized the Berkeley campus of the University of California in the 1960s. So Campus Crusade decided to introduce Jesus Christ at Berkeley. Six hundred Campus Crusade for Christ students were given the task to reach 27,000 Berkeley students with the gospel.

The students began with prayer, laboring over lists of Berkeley students' names, and strategizing how they would tell them about Jesus. A banquet was held for athletes. Student leaders heard a Christian testimony from an Arizona

State senator over breakfast. And 8,000 students and faculty listened intently as Billy Graham told the story of Jesus at an outdoor rally. Hundreds responded to the invitation to place their faith in Christ.

The rally had sparked Bill's imagination.

Why not train thousands of Christians at the same time? Then, they could go out and introduce Christ to their city. Bill wondered what city would be a good testing ground. It was decided that Dallas, Texas was perfect. Staff members talked to Dallas city officials to work through plans. In the spring of 1972, 85,000 students and lay-people from around the United States and the world gathered at the Texas Cotton Bowl for Explo '72. Then, the 85,000 were sent out into the city. By the end of the week, thousands of people had responded to the gospel message.

At the closing ceremony, an inspired Joon Gon Kim, Campus Crusade for Christ's director in Korea, invited everyone to join him in two years in Seoul. 'Three hundred thousand will join you there!' he boldly claimed.

For the next two years, Dr. Kim was busy. He handled every detail. Korean Campus Crusade for Christ staff members bought tents for people to sleep in, received governmental permission, got 12,000 Korean churches involved, and even purchased thirty huge rice cookers to feed 5,000 meals at a time.

Bill flew in the night before Explo '74 opened, to participate in an all-night prayer meeting with 160,000 other people. Explo '74 became the largest evangelistic training event in history. Looking out over the crowd, Bill and Dr. Kim estimated that 330,000 Korean college and high school students, lay-people and pastors had come to learn how to tell people about Jesus Christ. Over the next year, more than 300,000 Koreans took the gospel to their nation. By the year 2,000, it was estimated that 50% of Korea called themselves Christian. It was 20% in 1974. Something had happened!

When Bill left Korea, his mind raced with ideas.

Dr. Kim had inspired Bill. If Dr. Kim could reach Korea, then Bill wanted to reach the United States. Grabbing a piece of paper, he did some quick calculations. They would need large-scale outreaches in 265 major U.S. cities. It was no longer a question of if they could do it but how.

At Bill's side was MIT graduate, Steve Douglass. He was making Campus Crusade for Christ more efficient. Skeptics challenged this new idea of Bill's, but Steve kept it marching forward. They called it, 'Here's Life, America.' Their slogan was simple: 'I found it!' Radio ads, buttons and flyers were created. Pastors were challenged to lead campaigns in their cities. Volunteers were inspired to join the venture. In the end, 246 cities participated, with millions hearing the good news of Jesus Christ.

Whether it was a taxi-cab driver, or a United States senator, Bill Bright continued to tell them about Jesus Christ. His own fresh experiences inspired those around him.

Bill used whatever means were available to promote Jesus Christ. Sometimes, that meant stepping into the political arena. In 1983, Bill Bright joined President Ronald Reagan as he signed the 'Year of the Bible' proclamation. In 1988, Bill supported Vonette when she founded the National Prayer Committee and serve as the chairperson for the National Day of Prayer Task force. Bill beamed with pride when, because of Vonette's efforts, an unanimous act of Congress signed by President Reagan established a National Day of Prayer for the United States.

Other ideas were controversial. In the early 1990s, Bill signed a document with leaders of the Catholic church, highlighting what they agreed about rather than disagreed about. Bill knew many Catholics who were believers, particularly in the church worldwide. Desiring to throw open those doors so that even more could hear the good news of Jesus Christ, Bill signed the document. Though it roused controversy, still Bill was not shaken. He was gripped by the vision of reaching the world with the gospel of Jesus Christ.

Other ideas took years for fulfillment.

One idea had simmered for two decades. Bill wanted to produce a film about Jesus. But he waited until God gave him the green light. In those years of waiting, God brought the pieces together.

John Heyman was a successful film producer. His credits included *Grease, Chinatown,* and *Saturday Night Fever.* Despite his success, John was fed up. He was tired of actors who behaved like children. He was weary of the greed that drove studios. There must be something more, he thought. He suddenly wondered if he would find answers in the Bible. He began to read it. Soon, John was inspired to capture the book on film. He started with the book of Genesis, filming the stories in the first twenty-two chapters with great attention to detail. Then, he moved to the book of Luke to tell the story of Jesus. John soon realized he had run out of money. Where might he find the money to produce such a film, he wondered? He picked up the phone.

A few hours later, Bill hung up his phone, beaming. He had just received a phone call from the young Hollywood producer. He sat back in his chair, before slipping to his knees, thanksgiving flowing from his heart. At last, God

117

was answering his long-time desire and prayer. Someone wanted to produce a film on the life of Christ.

Bill prayed for John; for a staff person to take on responsibility, for funds; for the actors to be selected; and most of all, for the audiences who would watch it.

Rising, Bill knew who should take charge of the project: Paul Eschleman. Bill had asked Paul to take charge of Explo '72, and he had done well. He was now hard at work on the 'I Found It!' campaign. Bill asked his assistant to call Paul.

Paul was in the middle of a crisis. Things were not going well for the 'I Found It!' campaign in several cities. He and several national leaders of Campus Crusade had set the day aside for prayer. In the middle of the day, he received word that Bill Bright's assistant was on the phone. Bill wanted him to meet a man that day who had a Bible film for him to view. Paul told the assistant that he had no time. 'Perhaps another day,' Paul finished, before hanging up.

A few minutes later, the phone rang again. It was Bill Bright's assistant again. Instead of Paul driving into Hollywood, the assistant told Paul, Bill had arranged for the film producer to be sent to him. 'He will be there within the hour,' the assistant said simply, and hung up.

Paul didn't understand the urgency, but he greeted John Heyman, who arrived loaded down with a movie projector and canisters of film. 'I have to limit you to one half- hour,' Paul told him, 'We are in the middle of a crisis.'

John set up the projector. Impatient, Paul helped prepare the room. Then taking a seat, he folded his arms across his chest. But as the film played, Paul was undone. John had produced a refreshing and dramatic portrayal of Creation. The atmosphere changed. Paul realized this was something special. Bill Bright was on to something, he thought.

A few weeks later, Paul met John again. This time, John led the meeting. He took a deep breath and began. 'My parents came from Germany. I am a Jew. My father realized what Hitler was, and sent all of us away. He escaped on a bicycle a week before Hitler took power. Most of our relatives were gassed or killed in concentration camps.

'Through it all,' John continued, 'God was never mentioned. My father was in contact with some of the greatest philosophical minds of the day. But, again, never was God mentioned,' John paused, and added softly, looking down, 'And so, I know little of God. But I have two questions. First … how did you become a Christian? And second, why did you do it?'

Paul told John his story. Reaching into his pocket, he pulled out a yellow booklet, *The Four Spiritual Laws*. Paul explained the gospel to John, who interrupted from time to time to ask thoughtful questions. When Paul asked John if he wanted to respond to God's offer of salvation through Jesus Christ, John said, 'Of course, …'

'… But I can't,' he quickly added, 'That's a huge jump to take. I would be turning my back on the six million Jews who died in the Holocaust.'

Paul and John walked out to John's car, discussing John's obstacles. Reaching his car, John reached out and hugged Paul, surprising him. Over the next few months as they discussed the film's production, John continued to ask both Bill and Paul more questions. One year later, John responded to the gospel of Jesus Christ and became a believer.

Bill thought back to how God had been at work, not only in John, but also in the film. The script had been carefully written, based on Luke's gospel, and presented to 450 religious leaders, all of whom gave encouraging feedback and excellent suggestions of how to improve the script. Actors were selected. Locations were scouted out in Israel. Distribution plans were made with key religious leaders in the U.S. Then there was the need for money to produce the film. Hollywood studios had closed their ears to the idea. Bill invited John to join him at a weekend designed specifically to raise funds for evangelism projects. Christian businessmen and women were invited from all over the United States.

John told those at dinner of how he had become a Christian. He spoke softly and from his heart. He spoke of his questions, the meetings with Paul and Bill. He told of how he had met Jesus Christ, the son of the God of Abraham, Isaac and Jacob. Many hearts were moved that evening.

One woman in particular was touched by John's story. Caroline Hunt talked to her husband, Bunker about the film project. Before leaving that evening, they approached Bill about the project. By morning they had decided to underwrite the film, a three million dollar gift.

Even before the 'JESUS' film hit theatres, God used it to draw people to himself, actors, production assistants and a Warner Brothers top executive. It was Bill's idea but it was God who was working through it, to his glory.

The flight attendant picked up the cup from Bill's tray. She smiled, and told him they were about to land. Bill thanked her, and turned to Vonette. Bill began to pray. He praised God for his faithfulness, grace and love for men. He thanked God for the 'JESUS' film. But before Bill finished, he was already thinking ahead. Bill Bright began to pray that one billion souls would desire a relationship with Jesus Christ before the year 2000 A.D.

The Gospel for Anyone

Bill pushed the curtain back with the back of his hand. He peeked out to the large room. Moby Gym buzzed with activity. Fresh-faced, clean-cut men and women streamed into bleachers to find seats. Young mothers with strollers were lining the back of the hall. The praise and worship team stepped to the microphones. Bob Horner, who was leading the evening, jumped up onto the stage. Raising the microphone, he called a greeting to the crowd. He then invited the 5,000 men and women to stand and worship God.

It was the mid-1990s. Campus Crusade for Christ staff members had flooded onto Colorado State University's campus in Ft. Collins, Colorado for ten days. They would listen to speakers, receive training, participate in praise and worship, and hear reports of what God had done through their fifty different ministries.

As the praise and worship team began, the lights dimmed. Words to choruses appeared on three enormous screens. Singing filled the auditorium. The gym was now a chapel.

Bill pushed the curtain aside. Dressed classically in suit and tie, a white handkerchief crisply folded in his breast pocket, he escorted Vonette, who was festively adorned in red, to two seats on the front row near the stage. He hoped they had slipped in unnoticed.

Before closing his eyes to join the 5,000 voices united

in harmonious praise and worship of their great God, Bill turned to briefly survey the room.

'It's amazing what God has done,' he thought.

He loved this time. He loved the worship, hearing the stories of what God was doing. He loved being with his staff. The filled room was evidence that the vision he had received was from God. This was God's fulfillment. This was to God's glory.

After twenty minutes Bob was back up on stage. Known for his humor, and his bushy eyebrows, soon, through a series of his announcements, laughter filled the hall. Bob then turned and nodded at Bill. Bill reached over and grabbing his wife's hand, he whispered, 'It's time!'

As Bob introduced their president and founder, Bill and Vonette climbed the three stairs to the stage. A microphone was handed to Bill before they both turned to look at the eager sea of faces before them.

'Greetings in the matchless name of our Lord and Savior, Jesus Christ!' he called. Cheers rang in the gym, and Bill turned to Vonette, 'I am sure you know my bride, the lovely Mrs. Vonette Bright.' More cheers erupted in the room, as Vonette took the microphone from Bill.

'Well, hello, all!' Vonette waved, her Oklahoman warmth filling the corners of the room.

'You look beautiful this evening, dear,' Bill told his wife, seemingly oblivious to the thousands of eyes gazing at them.

'Why, thank you, honey,' Vonette replied, more aware of the audience than her husband. 'You look pretty good yourself.' Turning to the crowd, Vonette exclaimed, 'But don't they look good, too?'

Shouts and applause descended to the ceiling in response to Vonette's notice of the staff members.

This was family time. Bill and Vonette had begun telling staff members of the happenings of their own lives and family many years ago. Even though 5,000 sat before them, still this time was to be personal. Vonette began to describe the last two years. In response to her descriptions, Bill quipped with side comments and quick-witted responses. Gales of laughter rippled though the crowd. The 'Bright Family Hour' never disappointed. Bill and Vonette's banter was as real on stage as if they were standing in their own living room.

'Now, that's not true, dear,' Vonette reproachfully replied to one of her husband's quips, as Bob Horner approached the couple. Bill turned in welcome. 'Ah, Bob, good timing as usual.' Chuckles sounded again.

Addressing the staff members, Bob told the crowd that they would hear more from Bill and Vonette throughout the conference. At the moment, there were some special people who wanted to join them. On Bob's cue, Bill and Vonette retraced their steps. Finding their seats, they turned to see streams of high school students cheering loudly as they raced into the gym. They ran toward the stage.

Two students ran up on stage to join Bob. The teenagers had been out at an all-day rally with *Student Venture*, the Campus Crusade high school ministry. Bob turned to the young boy and the young girl, with interview questions in hand. 'Now, where have you two been?' he asked.

The students began to recount their 'awesome' day. 'There were really great games ... the bands were awesome! ... and Josh McDowell spoke ...' Bob interrupted, 'And what did Josh talk about?'

'Well, he talked about making right choices based on God's character,' the young girl began, but instantly blushing, she stopped, suddenly at a loss for words. Looking at the crowd, the young man grinned and said loudly, 'He talked about sex!'

Bob's eyebrows shot up. 'Really,' he said in mock surprise. 'Did you learn anything?' he queried, to laughter from the crowd. Both boy and girl blushed now.

'Okay, okay,' Bob broke in, rescuing the students from more embarrassment, 'Don't answer that. For someone who talks to thousands of people about Jesus Christ, Josh does seem to talk about sex a lot, doesn't he.' He grinned at the audience. 'Thank you, Becca and Todd!' The two students ran down the stairs, relieved to join their friends. 'Let's give them a hand!' he called to the crowd.

Bill smiled. The staff members of *Student Venture*, Josh McDowell and the music ministry bands who had played today shared his energy. They were loving students to Jesus.

As the clapping died away, Bob moved on to the next segment. 'You know, God has been at work. He has done some pretty amazing things in our movement over the last two years. Let's hear some of those stories.'

The lights faded. Bill gazed at the left-hand screen. The New York skyline appeared. Bill wondered which Campus Crusade ministry in New York this might be. *Here's Life Inner City* reached out to those in need of justice, food or clothing. The *Executive Ministry* reached out to men and women on Wall Street. Or, thought Bill, it could be about the *Christian Embassy* that worked at the United Nations, telling international representatives from all around the world about Jesus Christ.

Bill smiled as he recognized the staff person. During the Thanksgiving holidays, *Here's Life Inner City* staff members had taken food to thousands of families in need. Through their outreach, they showed the love of Christ in a way that people could see and touch. Astonishment shone on the faces of those who had received the food and the kindness in Jesus' name. It was a powerful ministry. Vonette grabbed Bill's hand. The screen faded. Whoops and clapping filled the gym. Bill looked at the right hand screen. A young woman appeared.

'Hello! My name is Dawn Burton. I'm a student at the University of Tennessee in Knoxville, Tennessee,' she began. Behind her, a diver jumped into an Olympic-size swimming pool. She had won the Southeastern Conference platform-diving title last year, she told the crowd. But, she continued, regardless if she was first or last, her real prize was knowing Jesus Christ.

Dawn told of meeting Kelly Eason, an *Athletes in Action* staff member. 'Kelly helped me be a part of what God was doing,' Dawn said, 'I became a Christian as a young girl, but through Kelly, I am now telling other women athletes about Christ.' Smiling, she added she now led a Bible study with a diver, a rower, a soccer player and a sprinter. 'Giving 100% to diving is just part of it,' she finished, 'I want to give 100% to Christ.'

Bill sat back in his chair. He silently thanked God for the athletes he had met, who used their status to tell others about Christ.

Obnoxious honking sounded throughout the room. Center screen, the sight of New York cabs speeding through Times Square appeared. 'Hi! I'm Cheryl Cutlip,' a tall young woman began, the honking fading, 'I'm a Christian ... who happens to be a Rockette.'

Cheers filled the gym. Ah, thought Bill, smiling again. Actors, dancers and singers in the entertainment industry were meeting Jesus Christ, too.

Dancing professionally in New York, Cheryl began, was not glamorous. It was hard work – eight-hour days, six shows a day – with 200 shows just for Christmas. Long hours and little sleep did not motivate Cheryl, she told the audience, but Christ did. She had the privilege of telling dancers about Jesus, she said. 'In fact, a woman named Rhonda just seemed to drink in the *Four Spiritual Laws* when she heard it for the first time.'

'Telling people about Christ in this industry is risky,' Cheryl continued, 'Unlike other professions, dancers eat, breathe and live in each other's space. Everything you do is watched critically. But I have big dreams for the dance community. I want to see the community be a witness for Jesus Christ. In the meantime …' Cheryl concluded, 'I will continue to keep Christ's light shining brightly here in New York.'

The screen faded and Bob returned to the stage.

'We first heard this story two years ago. We were introduced to this young man by staff members on campuses in Boston,' Bob began, unusually sober. 'I am speaking of Steve Sawyer, a young man from New Hampshire who met Jesus Christ while at Curry College in Boston. Steve was a haemophiliac. In the 1980s, Steve received a transfusion. Shortly after, he learned he was HIV-infected. It would lead to AIDS,' he said. 'Two years ago, Steve asked you to help him use his last years to tell people about Jesus Christ.'

Bob continued, 'You responded. You invited Steve to your campuses. Here's how God has used Steve,' he finished. The lights dimmed. On all three overhead screens, a snow-covered Boston skyline emerged. Steve's story was told of contracting AIDS, meeting Campus Crusade for Christ staff members, and placing his faith in Jesus Christ.

'I initially blamed God for my situation,' Steve Sawyer's face filled the screen. 'But eventually I realized, I wanted my last days to have an impact for Christ.'

A staff person from Louisiana State University told of Steve's visit to their campus. He spoke to 700 students about death, AIDS, and the hope that lived in him because of Jesus Christ. The event made the campus paper.

Finally, Steve appeared again. 'I've been able to speak at 100 colleges around the world. I've been able to tell 16,000 students about my relationship with Jesus Christ. Thank you for the opportunity,' Steve finished quietly.

Bill wiped his eyes. His heart ached for the boy's family, for Steve. But he was overwhelmed by this young man's courage and example in the face of death.

Suddenly, Bob Horner spoke, this time out in the crowd on a bleacher. 'It is my privilege to introduce Steve to you,' Bob said quietly as he turned to a thin young man seated beside him. He was dressed causally in jeans, a t-shirt and an unbuttoned oxford shirt and smiled when introduced.

Bill pulled out his handkerchief, and held it over his eyes. Vonette reached into her purse to grab tissues. Emotion swept the room. This was the first time many had seen Steve. Spontaneously, staff members stood, clapping hard. As they quieted, Bob turned to Steve and asked how he was doing.

'Well, by all medical standards, I should be dead,' Steve replied. He explained about his T-cell count and his condition.

'Tell us about the last two years,' asked Bob, softly.

'It's been amazing! I've had the opportunity to tell thousands about Jesus Christ. You know, if I had to get this disease that's killing me for that one person to understand that they can have a relationship with Christ, then it is worth it.'

[1] An area in a sports stadium where supporters sit

'Don't get me wrong, I have my moments,' Steve continued, 'There are days when my ankles swell up and I can't seem to stand. Days when my joints ache, or I come down with a fever,' Steve said quietly, 'But in light of eternity, telling people about Christ is all that matters.'

The words hung in silence in the room. Bill squeezed Vonette's hand. She nodded. Steve, too, had made his own contract with God.

Bob finished by praying for Steve. Then, standing, he closed the evening. 'We've heard amazing stories! We've come a long way from being on one college campus fifty years ago. We've got Rockettes,' Bob began, counting off his fingers, 'High school students ... evangelists who talk about sex,' Laughter erupted, 'Staff members in the inner city ... athletes ... and college students facing death with extraordinary courage because of Christ. Truly, the gospel is for anyone! Have a good night! We'll see you in the morning!' Bob finished, waving goodbye.

Bill tucked his handkerchief into his pocket. His assistant leaned over and told Bill the meeting was confirmed. Bill and Vonette would meet Steve Sawyer in a few moments. Bill nodded. His assistant gestured to a group of men and women moving through the crowd toward Bill. Patting his wife's hand, Bill rose to meet them.

All around the World

Bill stood on the platform. He gazed out on an audience of Russian men and women. These were not just average Russians, but some of the most influential in Moscow. Nine of Russia's eleven top cabinet ministers were in the audience. Bill was standing on the stage of the House of Filmmakers, a highly prestigious institution in Russian society. Paul Eschelman had invited Bill to introduce the 'JESUS' film, now dubbed in Russian. This was its premiere.

All 1,800 seats had been sold out. The organizers were forced to plan another showing the next day. Bill shuddered with joy. This was one of the greatest moments of his life, he knew. He was too excited to be nervous or shy. His mind raced back to 1947.

He had been at Forest Home with Miss Mears for a conference. She had invited Dr. Oswald J. Smith, a famous Canadian evangelist to speak. Dr. Smith placed a large map of the world in the front of the auditorium. Passionately, he persuaded the young adults to consider how they were personally going to reach the world for Jesus Christ. After his message, Dr. Smith walked over to the map. He invited each person to ask God what place on earth they would claim for Christ. Then, he motioned that the group should come forward. Reaching into his pocket, he pulled out a pen. Dr. Smith offered it to the crowd. 'Come and sign your name on the map on the location that you are led to pray over,' he instructed them.

Bill got out of his seat. He walked to the map, reached for the pen, and wrote his name over the Soviet Union. Ever since that night, through the Cold War, he had prayed that the Soviet republics would know the love of Christ.

Bill's memory skipped forward a couple of decades. By the late 1980s, it looked as if things were changing in Russia. Soviet President Mikhail Gorbachev's 'perestroika' and 'glasnost'[1] had initiated an avalanche of response from his people. By 1988, Bill and Campus Crusade staff began to investigate whether Russia was indeed opening its doors to the gospel. As promising as things had seemed, yet the Soviet Union still seemed closed. Paul Eschleman had tried hard to get the 'JESUS' film in, but to no avail. The Communist party blocked every move. On Paul's visits to Russia, the KGB followed him wherever he traveled. His rooms were bugged. Meeting Christian contacts meant spending an hour backtracking, changing vehicles, and meeting in public places away from listening ears. Undeterred, Bill and Vonette continued to pray.

Bill cleared his throat and looked out across the huge crowd - an answer to prayer indeed. Before he prepared to speak he allowed himself to focus on one last memory. It was amazing to think of how it had all started. Bill remembered one of Paul's many trips to Moscow where he had been sitting in his hotel room praying. He was out of ideas. God would have to provide a way. Suddenly an idea – a risky idea – was suggested. What if Paul took a backdoor approach? Before he knew it, Paul was on his way to the Republic of Georgia. He was going to try to get the 'JESUS' film on the black market.

Paul met with a man named Rezo, a Georgian film producer. Rezo decided to make a deal with Paul. He would

130 [1] A political movement which initiated change in the Soviet Union

dub and distribute the 'JESUS' film in the Georgian language. Paul signed a contract with him.

That evening, Paul met with local Christians to tell them of the film. They glanced nervously at one another. Noticing their anxiousness, Paul asked what was wrong.

'Did you not know that Rezo is KGB?' they asked Paul.

Surprised, Paul said no. Understanding their concern, Paul promised to protect them. He alone would deal with Rezo. As they parted, Paul thought that this time God seemed to have an unusual plan. Sixteen months later, the film was dubbed and ready for its premiere.

All 2,300 seats of the Philharmonic Hall in Tbilisi were filled with Communist Party and government officials. After a formal ceremony of both Georgian and American officials, the film was started. It was watched in complete silence.

At the film's conclusion, an invitation to begin a personal relationship with Jesus Christ was given. During the prayer of repentance, Paul heard the muffled sounds of people weeping throughout the theatre. At the film's conclusion, the audience rose as one to applaud.

The premiere in Georgia promised to open doors in Moscow. In faith, preparations were made. Two years later, the 'JESUS' film was dubbed and ready for distribution in Russia. Now, here they were... not in Georgia this time but in Moscow, the capital city of the Soviet Union.

Nodding to his interpreter that he was ready to begin, Bill greeted the audience warmly. He greeted them as an American, but also as a Christian. He told the crowd that the Russian people had been in his prayers for forty years. As Bill's interpreter quickly translated this last thought to the crowded hall, cheers and enthusiastic clapping erupted throughout the room.

Bill finished. Applause again filled the room. The crowd sensed Bill's affection for them. It shone on his face as well as in his words. He promptly returned to his seat. Ceremony was a necessary part of the event, but Bill was anxious for the film to start. Paul too, looked ready to get on with the main reason they were there…to introduce Jesus Christ to Russian men and women.

The film began. Bill prayed silently for the 1,800 gathered in the hall. He prayed for the salvation of those who did not know Christ personally. He prayed that the film would bring hope to a nation ravaged by seventy years of atheism and Communism. During the movie however, Bill became aware of movement in the crowd. A few viewers got up and left. One. Two. Bill started to count. More than ten left the hall. Bill turned back to the film, continuing to pray for the remaining viewers. As the film finished, an invitation to begin a personal relationship with Jesus Christ was given. The credits began to roll, and the audience clapped politely, remaining in their seats.

The clapping was reserved, Bill noted. He was surprised. At the Georgian premiere, Paul had told him of unbridled emotion and an outpouring of response for the film, and for Jesus Christ. His interactions with Russians since his arrival had also been warm, and passionate. He had taken every opportunity to talk about Jesus Christ with men and women he met. This lack of emotion was curious, he thought. He wondered what it meant. Paul looked disheartened as well. Bill saw Paul stop a Russian actress to ask her what she thought of the film.

'It was wonderful!' she responded. Paul asked if she thought most of the audience would agree. 'Yes, of course,' she told him.

'Then, why was the response so subdued,' Paul asked?

The woman gazed at Paul for a moment. 'You do not understand Russians,' she told him quietly. 'Those who watched the film were overwhelmed. They have never seen a movie about God. They are filled with many thoughts, as I am. Filled with thoughts that I have never had before.' It was a somber moment. Not one to be trivialized.

'You don't play drums after a prayer, do you?' she asked Paul, making her point, 'You will not see Russians clapping after a prayer.'

Paul and Bill began to talk to many of the viewers. They realized that the film had a powerful effect. Quiet tears filled many Russian eyes. But this was all new. Seventy years of fear held enthusiastic response captive.

As Bill left the hall to return to the hotel, he thanked God for a wonderful evening. He climbed into the back of the car. As he leaned back in his seat, looking out to a landscape of concrete block buildings and the occasional onion-domed church, Bill sensed this was only the beginning of what God had in store in Russia.

This wasn't the first time Bill had spoken to Russians about his Lord, Jesus Christ. Bill smiled as he remembered flying into Moscow in 1989. There he met two Russian scientists who were staying at his hotel. He invited them to join him for dinner. Over the meal, Bill told the men that his mission was to see that all people be given the opportunity to know Jesus Christ personally. He told them story after story of how his mission was being fulfilled. One of the men asked Bill if he would be interested in taking his message about Jesus Christ to the people of Russia.

The other scientist nodded. Would Bill be willing to appear on Russian television to report this?

'Of course!' Bill responded.

The following morning at nine o'clock Bill was at a local television station to be interviewed for a government-produced Russian news special. As the interviewer and Bill settled into chairs, the reporter commented that Soviet President Mikhail Gorbachev and American President George Bush, Sr. were at a summit in San Francisco that same week. He asked Bill his opinion about President Bush and the approaching summit. Bill, who had spent time at the White House days earlier, answered the question and added that he knew from personal conversation that President Bush read his Bible and prayed.

The interviewer sat up. The interview had just taken a turn. The connection between Bill Bright and the American president changed everything. He fired questions at Bill. When they finished, the reporter excitedly informed Bill that the interview would not be aired as originally suggested. Instead, it would be part of an hour-long special about the summit.

The program aired a few days later. It featured President Gorbachev, President Bush and Bill Bright. An estimated 150 million viewers across the Soviet Union heard Bill talk about God, Jesus Christ, faith, prayer, the Bible and the 'JESUS' film.

Bill's mind flew to the other opportunity he had had when invited to give an Easter message to 5,000 people at the Palace of Congresses in Moscow. The Easter message was televised and reached an estimated 150 million homes. Again, Bill spoke warmly of his Savior and Lord, Jesus Christ.

These were good memories, Bill thought. He wondered what other memories, good ones, would result from this particular trip to the Soviet Union.

Paul hastened over to Bill. Excitement was written all over his face. Paul had news for Bill. The Russian Minister of Education had offered to place the 'JESUS' film in 43,000 Russian schools if Campus Crusade for Christ would finance the project. In addition, Paul would be allowed to train the teachers to show the film, and to teach their children about Christianity.

Bill could not contain his excitement. Forty years of prayer were now being dramatically answered. Immediately, Bill knew that he and Vonette would want to help finance this venture. After he and Vonette talked it over, they decided to give $50,000 from their retirement account to help get the 'JESUS' film into Russian schools. What better investment could they make, they thought? Besides, God would take care of them, Bill knew. He always did.

By the time Paul and his team had trained 23,000 teachers, it became apparent to Bill that the openness in the Soviet Union was creating more opportunities than they could handle on their own. Thousands were responding to Christianity, desperate to fill the spiritual emptiness left by Communism. Bill knew they needed help. The opportunities might not always be there and they had to act quickly.

His own staff members were doing all that they could to reach into the Soviet republics with the gospel message. Hundreds of Campus Crusade for Christ staff had been traveling to Russia.

Athletes in Action basketball teams, wrestling teams, even football teams were going to Russia to play against Russian athletes, and during intermission were telling the crowds about Jesus Christ. Josh McDowell and his staff were heading up 'Operation Carelift' in order to bring hundreds of Christian helpers and tons of humanitarian aid for orphans, school children and military families. *Christian Leadership*, a Campus Crusade for Christ ministry to professors was taking American professors to Russia to tell their Russian academic colleagues about Christ. And hundreds of staff members were moving their families to Russia for two years to help train Russian schoolteachers who were teaching ethics and morality in remote village schools.

Bill began to discuss the need in the Soviet Union with other Christian ministries. They were agreed. This was an unprecedented opportunity. Joining under the umbrella of the newly created 'Co-Mission,' 80 church and para-church groups linked arms. Together they would reach the former Soviet Union with the gospel of Jesus Christ.

Prayer and Fasting

The Bible lay open on Bill's bed. Its worn leather and creased pages now opened readily to a particular page. It was a passage he had been meditating on often for the last few months… *Then if my people who are called by my name will humble themselves and pray and seek my face and turn from their wicked ways, I will hear from heaven and will forgive their sins and heal their land (II Chronicles 7:14 NLT).*

Campus Crusade for Christ had recently moved its headquarters to Orlando, Florida. Many people whispered that it was because Bill Bright wanted to retire in Florida. Nothing could be further from the truth. Bill had never considered retiring. How could you retire from telling people of the love of God through Jesus Christ?

It was a sad day when he and Vonette closed the door to their bungalow at Arrowhead Springs. They had lived there for twenty-nine years. They had raised sons there. They had raised their staff family there. They had spent many hours on their knees together in that bungalow. Memories called out to them as they stood, arm in arm, by their little home.

But they knew they needed to go. Campus Crusade had once again outgrown its facilities. The vision Bill had in 1951 still drove the ministry. They were to reach the whole world with the gospel of Jesus Christ in this generation.

It had taken them two years to find the right location, but finally Orlando was selected. Bill envisioned a World Center for Evangelism and Discipleship, a place dedicated to fulfilling the goal of reaching the entire generation with the gospel of Jesus Christ.

Bill now felt the aches and pains of age more readily. But this made him focus even more on reaching the world with the gospel. However, it would not happen without the power of the Holy Spirit at work in the Christian church. 'The world is in great need. It needs great resources. And America has been given so much,' thought Bill.

Sadness crept over his face as he thought about the United States. How rotten it had become, held in the grip of sin. But nothing was impossible with God, Bill thought. He picked up his Bible and turned to the book of Matthew. In chapter seventeen there was the story about the father who brought his son to Jesus for healing: *'Afterward the disciples asked Jesus privately, 'Why couldn't we cast out that demon?'*

'You didn't have enough faith,' Jesus told them. 'I assure you, even if you had faith as small as a mustard seed you could say to this mountain, "Move from here to there," and it would move. Nothing would be impossible. But this kind of demon won't leave unless you have prayed and fasted.'

The last words really struck Bill and he slowly sank down on the edge of his bed, deep in thought. He had never read those words in that way before.

Prayer had been emphasized from day one in Campus Crusade for Christ. It was a vital part of the day. No matter where Campus Crusade staff worked, everyone spent several hours a week as groups or on their own in prayer for the ministry. In fact, they were now building the Prayer Center at the Headquarters and Vonette had helped establish the National Day of Prayer.

But this was different. Bill looked down at the words on the page again. *'... unless you have prayed and fasted.'*

Bill had fasted for a few days but never longer. He thought of examples of fasting in Scripture. He thought about Jesus' fast of forty days. Bill had never fasted for forty days before. But never had he felt urgency like this either. Consulting physicians and books on the topic, Bill decided he would fast for forty days. He would begin his fast at the beginning of July. He would drink only water and fruit juices.

It was not easy. Bill was still traveling 300 days out of the year. It was a physical challenge. It involved much sacrifice. He loved food ... sweets especially. And it took a toll on his energy. But he soon realized the forty day fast was revolutionizing his relationship with God. He sensed God's presence. Not eating allowed Bill more time to spend alone with God. As the days passed, Bill began to sense that God would bring about a great spiritual awakening – one of the greatest harvests in Christian history.

It was Day Twenty-nine. Bill was again reading II Chronicles chapters 20-30. Sinful, evil leaders led Judah. The results were devastating. The Jewish people no longer acknowledged God or worshipped Him. Bill saw a parallel with his own nation.

He read on. A new king was established. King Hezekiah was crowned. In one of his first acts, King Hezekiah re-opened the doors of the temple that his own father had nailed shut. He then cleaned it out and sent letters to the whole kingdom calling for the people to return to worship. Bill asked God to show him how to apply the meaning of the passage to America. Slowly, he realized that it was not the political arena that must be cleaned up. 'It is the leadership of the church!' he exclaimed.

Eleven days later, armed with an image of a letter writing Jewish king, Bill began to write letters. He had a plan. First,

Dare to be Different

Bill wrote to a group of renowned Christians to join him sponsor a time of fasting and prayer for the leadership of the Christian church in the United States. He did not want this to be a Campus Crusade for Christ event. He wanted it to be an event for Christian leaders. Two dozen leaders agreed to join him in hosting the time. On behalf of this group, Bill wrote to hundreds of Christian influencers throughout the States. He invited them to come to Orlando, hotel expenses paid, to pray and fast for three days.

The invitation was simple, as was the program. They would fast and pray. Their nation was in crisis. Its people were in need of forgiveness. And the Christian church needed to come together to humble itself and seek God's face. Bill began to pray that 300 people would come.

More than 600 showed up and as they entered the enormous ballroom of the hotel, something was different. There was no stage. There were no fancy brochures. One single microphone stood before the room.

Bill began the time by handing out sheets of paper and pens. He asked the group to begin with a time of confession. The group was invited to write down any and all sins that came to mind. They were encouraged to do this individually, silently, and with great thought and prayer.

The room grew still, silence broken only by the sound of pen meeting paper. After a long time, Bill finally stood up. In a quiet voice, he said, 'Please write across your paper, "The blood of Jesus Christ cleanses us from all sin."'

With his Bible in hand, he asked the group to find I John 1:9. He encouraged each person to write the promise over his or her personal list of sins. *'But if we confess our sins to him, He is faithful and just to forgive us and to cleanse us from every wrong.'*

Bill led the group in prayer asking God for the power of

the Holy Spirit and personal revival. Bill then asked the group to do something that had not been seen in years. Pointing to the microphone in front of him, he invited everyone to come forward to it. They were not to come, said Bill, to tell of the accomplishments of their individual ministries. Nor, were leaders to preach or share a message with the group.

'No,' Bill said quietly, 'the microphone is here for you to make public confession of your sins to your brothers and sisters in the room. It might be that you have lost your first love for Jesus. It might be pride. It might be moral impurity. Sexual impurity. Materialism. It might be that you have neglected your family. It might be racism or a critical attitude.'

Bill surveyed the group, with affection in his eyes, 'We all sin, don't we? You know your individual sins. I invite you to confess them. I invite the leaders of the American church sitting here today to humble themselves, and pray. I invite you, the American church leadership, to seek God's face, turn from your wicked ways,' Bill continued, 'And God will hear from heaven, forgive our sin and heal our land.'

Bill stared out at the group. He did not know how this would go. He left the microphone and sat down. Slowly at first, one at a time, leaders of the American church walked forward to the microphone. Before the sea of 600 faces, each recounted sins that had gripped their hearts. One confessed that his denomination had not dealt with the racism in their church. Another leader confessed that his love of money was often part of his decision-making. Another confessed he loved to be busy more than he loved spending time with his Lord. Many declared they had not prayed for the nation's political leaders. Instead they had condemned those leaders when their sin became widely known.

For three days, the group of 600 confessed sin to each other. They wept together. In smaller groups, they prayed for one another. They read Scripture to each another on God's view of sin, of His forgiveness through the blood of Jesus Christ. They sang praises to God. They often prayed to God to forgive their land and heal it.

By the third day, the group was lifted with fresh faith and peace. New ideas began to surface. Bill encouraged others to fast and pray as he had. Others tried to work out how to go back to their denominations and organizations and pass on what they had learned and experienced.

Many had come to realise that they did not pray for the leaders of the land so a letter was drawn up and signed by the group where they promised to pray for the nation's leadership. In it, they also urged America to confess her sins. The letter was sent to the president of the United States, the vice-president, leaders of the House and Senate, the Supreme Court justices and Joint Chiefs of Staff.

The conference ended. But Bill had just begun.

Immediately, Bill and his staff began preparing a larger prayer and fasting event for the following year. More than 4,000 would attend this event. Bill began to pray that 2 million Americans would join him in forty-day fasts for revival. Over the course of the next four years and using satellite link-ups, 2 million participants worldwide would come together to fast and pray.

Bill kept looking ahead. He had more work to do. He was planning to spend the rest of his years in prayer and fasting and continuing to reach the world with the gospel of Jesus Christ.

Going Home

Bill adjusted the oxygen tube. From his upper lip the tube continued over both ears and rested behind them like a pair of glasses. The tubes led to an oxygen tank that sat on the back of a wheelchair that Bill used often now. It slowed his physical mobility, he admitted. But that was it. It did not slow his mind or his heart.

He had been diagnosed with pulmonary fibrosis. The doctor told him his lungs would slowly lose their elasticity. And one day his lungs would deflate. No more air would be able to fill him. There was also no cure. When Vonette once asked him why God would allow him to suffer in such a painful way, Bill reminded her that compared to what Jesus Christ went through this was minor. It was a matter of perspective, Bill told her. Really, it was a privilege.

The disease had claimed 60% of his lung capacity when he had stepped down from the presidency of Campus Crusade for Christ in 2001. His friend of thirty-three years, vice-president Steve Douglass had been named president. Since that time, Bill had accomplished much. And he was so glad. He had written more. Published more. Launched more new endeavors. It had been good. But now there was another project. There was urgency in him to complete this one last thing. He wanted to give those he would leave behind a perspective from eternity. He pulled out his tape-recorder for dictation, and gasping for another breath, with great effort began: '*My beloved family, friends, staff members and partners in the gospel: I embrace you with the love of Christ. I want to share some things with you because I love you. Even in my death the Holy Spirit can use me to glorify the Father. I would be remiss not to share what He wants. So, thank you for these moments.'*

Bill put down the tape player. He pulled out a handkerchief and wiped his eyes. He had thought about death often. He thought about heaven more. He longed to be with his Lord. He could not help but tell friends when they called that despite the pain in breathing, he was praising the Lord. If he remained on earth for a time, he would still serve the Lord. If he died, he would be in heaven with Him. That would be magnificent! Either way, he couldn't lose.

It saddened him to think that Vonette would be separated from him. And his two sons ... their families ... his friends ... and dear staff family. He began to think about Christ and what he had done for him. This gave him joy but concern flooded his heart again. 'I hope I will not displease the Lord as I enter into the more difficult stages of this disease! When it gets tough will I remain godly? Perhaps I will cry out in bitterness at the pain? I pray that I will remain faithful to praise the Lord!' Bill put the handkerchief back into his pocket. He picked up the tape-recorder again. Reflecting for a moment, he then pushed the record button.

'First, I am now experiencing what I have longed for ever since I met Jesus in 1945, when I asked Him into my heart. I fell in love with Him deeply as He revealed Himself to me through His Word. For all these decades my greatest joy has been being in His presence and serving Him alongside Vonette. Today I am experiencing God face to face in ways so magnificent that they cannot be described in words. For 'no eye has seen, no ear has heard, no mind has conceived what God has prepared for those who love Him' (I Corinthians 2:9).

Bill thought of the deep ways he had experienced God in the past ten years. His first forty day fast had been such a rich experience that he had undertaken seven more since that first time. Indeed, only greater things were ahead for those who knew the Lord. The forty days fasts were but a glimpse of the personal revival to come when finally in the presence of the Lord in glory.

'So I offer you the same advice that Jesus offered His disciples in John 14:28 when He said they should rejoice at His going to be with the Father. Rejoice with me because I am no longer in this earthly tent. I am in the presence of the living God, satisfied at the deepest core of my being. And rejoice with me because I have finished all He called me to do. It has been a magnificent adventure to serve alongside my precious Vonette for over 50 years. Together we have raised two sons who love God. They, their godly wives and our four grandchildren have been our joy.'

Once again, Bill put down the recorder. He had grown weak and needed to rest a moment. He closed his eyes. Opening them a moment later, they rested upon a recent family picture. There was his beloved bride, Vonette sitting next to him. Brad was holding his young son, Keller. Brad's wife, Katherine was holding their daughter, Noel. Zac stood behind Bill and Vonette with his wife, Terry and their two children Rebecca and Christopher, both teenagers.

Zac and Brad were both in Christian ministry. Zac worked at a Presbyterian church in California. Brad had dabbled in politics but realized that politics could not change society. True change came from transformed hearts. Brad, then, decided to join Campus Crusade for Christ. Bill and Vonette were thrilled with both of their sons' decisions.

Bill's eyes now moved to the globe that stood in its stand across the room. God had accomplished much through

Campus Crusade for Christ in the last fifty years. It was now serving in 191 countries. Bill smiled. That was almost seventy more countries than McDonald's had reached. There were more than 26,000 full-time employees. There were more than 225,000 trained volunteers – eleven times the number of students at Harvard University. *The Four Spiritual Laws* had been printed into more than 200 languages, and distributed to more than 2.5 billion people.

'And then there is the 'JESUS' film,' Bill thought. 'It has been translated into 734 languages and viewed by more than 5.1 billion people, shown in every country of the world. In fact, the film has been into countries in where we have no staff representatives: its own little missionary.'

But it wasn't the numbers that inspired Bill. It was the transforming love of God that he had experienced in his own life. It compelled him to sit in taxi upon taxi telling the drivers the message of God's love. Bill communicated with everyone from hotel worker to flight attendant.

Feeling strength to continue, Bill leaned forward. He began to record with renewed energy. This next message was for those who did not know Christ.

'God has laid a message on my heart for you all. For you not yet believers: Seriously look at the magnificent offer of love and forgiveness that God extends you. Before this day is over, receive Jesus as your Savior and Lord. Consider that God loves you and offers a wonderful plan for your life. Take seriously that because each of us is sinful and separated from God, we cannot know and experience God's love and plan. Know that Jesus Christ is God's only provision for man's sin. Through Him you can know and experience God's love and plan for you. Finally, you must individually receive Jesus Christ as Savior and Lord; then you can know and experience God's love and plan. Those four points are the

heart of God's good news to humanity. If you do not yet know Jesus
Christ personally, please consider those points.

These were the basics. Throughout his life, Bill had
remained committed to simple principles. Bill was called
to love Jesus Christ and surrender his life, a slave for Jesus.
He was to confess sin moment by moment and be filled
with the Holy Spirit. In obedience, he was called to reach
the world with the gospel of Jesus Christ.

He thought back to the last staff conference in Colorado.
Brad had pushed his wheelchair to the microphone so that
he might be able to address the staff. Tied to his oxygen
tubes, he still managed to stand. It took every ounce of
strength, but he was determined to call them again to
remember their first love, Jesus Christ and then, 'to reach a
lost world for Christ!' he said once more in a now raspy
voice.

Moving the recorder to his other hand, Bill now shifted
focus: *'For you who know Jesus Christ personally I have a word for
you: Do not settle for mediocrity. You are a child of the God of the
universe. Surrender to Him. Become His slave. I can assure you,
after more than 50 years of experience, there is no greater adventure
than following Him. He cares for you. Take Him at His Word.*

*When Vonette and I signed a contract in 1951 to become slaves
of Jesus, we did so with the utmost confidence that 'everyone who
has left houses or brothers or sisters or father or mother or children
or fields for [His] sake will receive a hundred times as much and
will inherit eternal life' (Matthew 19:29). It made perfect sense
that since He created the heavens and the earth, died on the Cross
for our sins, and is obviously far more intelligent than we, His ways
are better than ours. So we turned everything over to Him. I can say
unequivocally that you will find no greater joy than in total
surrender.*

Dare to be Different

At the time Bill began his forty day fast to humble himself before God, without his knowledge he was being nominated for several awards. The timing was uncanny. Bill glanced around. Evidence of those awards now sat on shelves throughout the room. He had been inducted into the State of Oklahoma Hall of Fame. He had received the Gold Medallion Book Award for *Witnessing Without Fear*. And then there was the Templeton Prize for Progress in Religion. It was the world's largest annual prize, valued at $1 million dollars.

But he and Vonette had signed everything away in 1951. The Templeton Prize money went straight to promoting fasting and prayer throughout the world. Bill and Vonette felt they received far more back when they heard the reports of thousands who responded to Jesus Christ.

Bill received accolades from politicians, presidents, royalty and prominent Christians. But it would be seven words only he longed to hear from his one true king, 'Well done, my good and faithful servant.'

Bill cleared his throat. He was almost done. *'Finally, I want to pray for you. For you who know Jesus, I pray you would follow Jesus as a fully surrendered slave. And for you not yet following Jesus but considering the four points I shared earlier, I pray you would invite Christ to forgive your sin so you can begin a relationship with Him.*

'If someone needed to meet the Savior or be encouraged to walk with Him more intimately, then I didn't want to waste the opportunity. What I have believed by faith I am now experiencing in reality. I now see my Savior with my own eyes and I hear him with my own ears as I worship Him in a way I have never understood. This is a good day for me. I pray it will be a good one for you. God bless each of you.

It was a warm summer night in July. Once again, more than 5,000 Campus Crusade for Christ staff members had descended upon Colorado State University for the 2003 U.S. Staff Conference. Moby Gym was packed. Air conditioners blew cool air into the overcrowded gymnasium. The Saturday evening session had just begun.

Bill had said his goodbye to the staff at the staff conference two years earlier. But by God's grace and to the surprise of the medical community, he had remained to continue serving his Lord for two more years.

Bill's health had been declining. Vonette was updating staff members by e-mail that summer, letting everyone know that Bill's time was waning. He requested that Scripture be read to him, even when his medicine caused him to fall asleep. He continued to pray that he would remain godly even through the most torturous moments of his illness.

As the speaker made concluding remarks to the crowd in Moby Gym, Steve Douglass was tapped on the shoulder. His assistant whispered in his ear. He nodded. As the speaker stepped off the platform, Steve rose and climbed the stairs to the microphone. Earlier that evening, Steve had felt compelled to pull out a pad of paper and begin to prepare a few notes to say in case news came of Bill's death. In fact, at the beginning of the week, the leadership had continued to earnestly pray that Bill would be healed.

By Friday morning, however, they began to sense they needed to let Bill go. Shedding many tears and unclenching the tight grip with which they held their leader, they began to pray that God would take Bill home.

Steve stood before the staff. He surveyed the room, his family. 'At 7:25 p.m.,' Steve began, looking down at his notes, and then lifting his head, 'Bill Bright drew his first deep breath of celestial air.' Tears glistened in his eyes as the words came home to his own heart.

Muffled weeping could be heard throughout the gym. The staff prayed together. They wept. They comforted one another. And through their tears, they also worshipped God who had released their leader from his aching body. Bill was now worshipping more fully and deeply than he had ever imagined.

Everyone appreciated God's perfect timing. Bill loved the staff conference. He had often remarked that it was one of his favorite times. It seemed fitting that his staff family from around the United States would be gathered together when Bill went home to be with his Lord.

Two days later, a staff family memorial was held. It was a time to grieve together and celebrate Bill's life. To the surprise of many, Vonette flew to Colorado instead of remaining in Orlando. She wanted to be with the staff family.

That Monday night, Vonette stepped to the podium. She wore Bill's necklace of the Star of David with the cross of Jesus Christ. And, at a final request of her husband, she wore red. Vonette looked radiant. She was indeed experiencing God's peace, His comfort, and His grace. She told of Bill's final days. She spoke of what had been on Bill's heart up to the very last breath. Their son, Brad joined her in expressing gratitude in being able to say their final goodbyes. Several prominent Christian leaders also shared their remembrances of their final words with Bill.

Two weeks later on July 30, a memorial service was held for Bill Bright in Orlando, Florida. Dr. James Dobson, Rev. Pat Robertson, Chuck Colson, Dr. Charles Stanley, Dr. Robert Reccord, former Sen. William Armstrong, Dr. Adrian Rogers and John Maxwell participated. All were well-known, respected Christians who had known and worked alongside Bill for years.

It had been a topic of conversation for the couple for years. It was one Vonette refused to discuss. It was one that Bill had definite opinions about. If he died before Christ returned, Bill told Vonette, he wanted to be buried in an unmarked grave. The only opinion Vonette gave was that she didn't like the idea.

They would need to hear from God on this, they decided.

After much prayer, Vonette and Bill knew what to do. On their tombstone, it would read, 'Slaves for Jesus,' a reference to the Scripture verses that had inspired them for years: Philippians 2:7 and Romans 1:1. Bill wanted to challenge everyone who would visit the cemetery to become a slave for Jesus. Bill had considered slavery to Jesus his greatest privilege.

Vonette and Bill had shared fifty-four years, seven months and twenty days together. Before he died, Bill made sure to tell as many people as he saw to keep Vonette busy after he was gone. She had often said that the minute Bill had gone, she, too, wanted to die. But during Bill's sickness, God began to change Vonette's heart. A desire to remain and serve her Lord quietly filled her. She would carry on.

Perhaps it was what Bill had once written to her that God used to inspire the change: *I pray that when you and I go to be with the Lord, it will be said of us that we were faithful servants and that our lives produced great fruit for the glory of God. The only legacy of true value is a spiritual legacy.'*

Thinking Further Topics

1. Growing Up

Bill's family made lasting impressions on him. Bill's father taught him to work hard. His grandfather showed him courage. His mother took him to church, and showed him compassion in action. Think about your family. How has each person influenced you? Do you influence others? How?

2. Finding a Voice

Bill discovered many things he enjoyed doing, and did well. What do you enjoy doing? What do you do well? God has created us with our own gifts and talents. Read Psalm 139:13-14 and Ephesians 2:10. What does this say about how you have been created? What should we do with what God has given us?

3. Westward Bound!

Bill had a list of goals. He had plans. But he was disappointed when he couldn't join the military. Have you had disappointment when something didn't go your way? How did you respond? Read Romans 8:28. What will God do? Does that change how you feel? Have you ever thought how bad things can fit into God's purpose?

4. Meeting Miss Mears

Bill met Jesus through reading the Bible, the prayers of his mother and Miss Mears. Acts 6:5-12; 7:51-8:3; 9:1-19 tells the story of Paul. What was Paul's life like before and after meeting Jesus? Does Jesus live in you? How would you tell your story of how you met Jesus? If Jesus does not live in your life, write down: Who are you, Lord? What do you want with my life? Then, go to a quiet place, get on your knees, and ask God those two questions.

5. Becoming Expendable

Bill learnt that becoming a Christian involves learning how to serve and telling God about your sin. He learned the importance of studying Scripture and prayer and how to tell others about Christ. Being a Christian meant being faithful with responsibilities, being Jesus' representative to others. Read Colossians 1:9-10. How should you please God? Do you need help?

6. Vonette Zachary

Bill prayed to God and thought Vonette was the woman he was to marry. But he realized that Vonette did not know Jesus. He was faced with a dilemma: Should they get married, with different goals, different thoughts about faith, different beliefs about Jesus? Read Psalm 37:4. What were Bill's desires? Did he 'delight' in the Lord? What things have you wanted badly? Have you ever had to choose between what God wants and what you want? What does God want us to do with our desires?

7. The Contract

Bill was learning what obedience meant. Read Philippians 2: 7-9. Jesus was so obedient that he died on a cross. He wanted to live on God's terms. If you were to write a contract like Bill and Vonette did, what things would you write down? Do you think this decision is made one time only, or does it need to be made over and over? Miss Mears once told her class: 'The greatest of a man's power is the measure of his surrender. It is not a question of who you are, or what you are, but whether God controls you.' Are you willing to surrender your life and live it on Christ's terms?

8. Jumping in with Both Feet

Bill prayed that God would use him. He and Vonette had submitted their lives to the Lord. They wanted to surrender their lives to God. The Holy Spirit was at work, but God also used their desires and skills to lead them to service. Read Exodus 35:30-35. What have you shown skill in doing? What have been some exciting places to serve? Have you asked God if He might use your skills?

9. Making It Simple

Bill didn't realize it, but he often told people the same things when he told them about Jesus. Bill also thought about what was important to his generation. He took things that people could relate to and used them to tell others about Christ. What is important to people today? What you would say to others about Jesus and the cross? Do your friends believe in God? In Jesus? Do they think they are sinful? What do they believe? Look at Bill's outline. Write out how you would tell someone about Jesus.

10. God Meeting Needs

Bill learned that faith is like a muscle. It grows with exercise, and the more we know of the faithfulness of God – the more we can trust Him. Read Matthew 6:25-34. Jesus reminds us we are not to be anxious about life because God cares for us. God meets our needs. Is there a need in your life that you want God to meet? What do you know about God that will increase your faith? II Corinthians 5:7 says, 'we walk by faith, not by sight.' Bill realized the best way to express his faith was to thank God. Can you thank God, even when you don't know the outcome of a situation?

11. Big Vision, Big Faith

Bill learned how important it is to understand who God is. Scripture tells us about God's character. Look at the following verses? He is your protector (II Thessalonians 3:3); your Father (Isaiah 9:6; Deuteronomy 32:6); here forever (Revelation 22:13); good (Psalm 135:3); loving (I John 4:16; John 3:16); all-knowing (Psalm 94:9,11; Psalm 139:1-4, 15; II Chronicles 16:9); wise (Proverbs 3:19; Romans 11:33); sovereign (Psalm 47:2,8); able (Jeremiah 32:26-27); patient (II Peter 3:9; Psalm 103:8); near (Psalm 73:28; Psalm 145:18); rich (Psalm 50:10-12); strong (Psalm 62:2; Psalm 94:22); your refuge (Psalm 62:8); forgiving (Psalm 103:12; Psalm 130:4); your Creator (Jeremiah 32:17); and holy (Isaiah 6:3). How can you be involved in God's kingdom? Spend time with God. Ask him to give you an idea, like he gave Bill, that he might fulfil through you one day.

12. The Gospel for Anyone

Campus Crusade spread to inner cities, high schools, athletes, performers. Do you reach out to all people? Do you need to be a certain type of person to tell a particular group about Jesus? Do you need to be rich to tell a wealthy person about Jesus? Does a person's race, gender, social standing, or wealth matter? What does James 2:1-9 say about partiality? Jesus met a variety of people: fishermen (Luke 5:8-9); Pharisees (Luke 5:17; 11:37); tax collectors (Luke 5:27; 19:2-5); centurions (Luke 7:6-10); a young girl (Luke 8:41-42 & 54); a lawyer (Luke 10:25); a Samaritan

(Luke 17:16); and a thief (Luke 23:42-43). Do you believe the gospel is for anyone? Make a list of different people in your life. Can you tell them about Jesus Christ?

13. All Around the World

In 1947, Bill wrote his name over the Soviet Union on a map. He prayed that God would make it possible for its citizens to learn about Christ. Take out a map. Put your name on a place to pray for. Ask God to give you opportunity to bring the gospel of Jesus Christ to that nation. You may go there one day, or support a child who lives there, or pray regularly for it.

14. Fasting and Prayer

Bill Bright once said, 'Let your mind race. Let your prayers be without limit; and yet, whatever you believe, whatever you think, whatever you pray for — God's power is infinitely beyond it all.' Have you ever prayed impossible prayers — things that you think God will never answer? Do you ever feel as though your prayers are blocked? Prayer shows that you need help, doesn't it? Ultimately, when we pray to God, we are telling him that we need him. God is all-powerful. He cares for us. If we are Christians, we have direct access to God because Jesus died for us. Other times, there is sin in our hearts that we need to confess. Find a quiet place. Take a pen and ask God to point out your sin or unbelief. Now, write down the list. Take a different colored pen and write I John 1:9 over the list: *'But if we confess our sins to him, He is faithful and just to forgive us and to cleanse us from every wrong.'* Tell God your biggest dreams, even if they seem ridiculous. You may be surprised at what he will do!

15. Going Home

Bill Bright wanted to hear seven words, 'Well done, my good and faithful servant.' Death may seem like a long time away, but if you looked at your life right now, what do you think God would say? Read II Timothy 4:7-8. What does running the race look like? Write down two or three ideas of what running the race for Christ in your life would mean. If you were to write out what you would want on your tombstone, what would it say?

Prayer Suggestions:

1. Pray for people in authority and with influence: Church and national leaders; actors; athletes; musicians; business men and women. Thank God for them and for good role models.

2. Pray for family and friends: about their problems and concerns. Pray that God will bring you all to love and trust him. Thank God for teaching you about himself and for giving you his word

3. Pray for suffering humanity: The homeless, unemployed, drug addicts, Aids sufferers, bereaved, families of people who are sick. Thank God for family. Thank God for his care of you and them.

4. Pray for the persecuted church: those who do not have the freedom to worship Jesus publicly or to read the Bible; people who are in prison for their faith. Thank God for your freedom and for the ability to read and hear God's word.

5. Pray for Campus Crusade for Christ and its workers. Thank God for all the different Christian organisations you know which work to help people and spread God's word.

6. Pray for yourself; that God will give you spiritual discipline and a desire to love and worship him. Thank God for your abilities, your personality, all the good things that make you unique!

7. Pray for the Church and the cause of Christ. Pray that people around the world will hear the good news of Jesus. Thank God for the life of Bill Bright and other people who gave their lives to spread the gospel.

Page 57: [1]Cited by Bill Bright, *The Secret - How To Live With Purpose and Power*, New Life Publications, 1999, 2003, Orlando, Fla., p. 11; from *That Strong Name,* James Stewart, Edinburgh, Scotland.

Page 60: Michael Richardson. *Amazing Faith: How One Man Spent His Life Taking God at His Word*. (Colorado Springs, CO: Waterbrook Press, 2000), 36.

Page 62: Michael Richardson. *Amazing Faith: How One Man Spent His Life Taking God at His Word*. (Colorado Springs, CO: Waterbrook Press, 2000), 37-38.

Trailblazers

Heroes to look up to!

Corrie ten Boom,
The Watchmaker's Daughter
ISBN 1 85792 116X

Joni Eareckson Tada,
Swimming against the Tide
ISBN 1 85792 833 4

Adoniram Judson,
Danger on the Streets of Gold
ISBN 1 85792 6609

Isobel Kuhn, Lights in Lisuland
ISBN 1 85792 6102

C.S. Lewis, The Story Teller
ISBN 1 85792 4878

Martyn Lloyd-Jones,
From Wales to Westminster
ISBN 1 85792 3499

George Müller, The Children's Champion
ISBN 1 85792 5491

John Newton, A Slave Set Free NEW
ISBN 1 85792 834 2

John Paton, A South Sea Island Rescue
ISBN 1 85792 852 0

Mary Slessor, Servant to the Slave
ISBN 1 85792 3480

Hudson Taylor, An Adventure Begins
ISBN 1 85792 4231

William Wilberforce, The Freedom Fighter
ISBN 1 85792 3715

Richard Wurmbrand, A Voice in the Dark
ISBN 1 85792 2980

Gladys Aylward, No Mountain Too High
ISBN 1 85792 5947

Bill Bright
Timeline

1920　Women granted the vote in the U.S.

1921　Bill Bright born

1922　Readers Digest published

1923　Talking Movies invented

1924　Lenin dies

　　　First Olympic Winter games

1927　BBC founded

1928　Bubble gum invented

1931　Empire State Building completed

1932　Scientists split the atom

1933　Franklin D Roosevelt launches New Deal

1934　Monopoly game goes on sale

1936　Hoover Dam completed

1938　Hitler annexes Austria

1939　World War II begins

　　　Bill Bright graduates from High School

1940　Battle of Britain

1941　Japanese attack Pearl Harbor

1945　World War II ends.

　　　Bill Bright becomes a Christian

1947　Dead Sea Scrolls discvoered

　　　Bill Bright prays for U.S.S.R.

1949　First non stop flight around the world

1950　First organ transplant

　　　Credit card invented

1951　Colour T.V. introduced.

　　　Campus Crusade founded

1952　Princess Elizabeth becomes Queen at age 25

1953	Hillary and Norgay climb Mt. Everest
	DNA discovered
1955	Rosa Parks refuses to give up her seat on a bus
1956	Bill Bright writes *The Four Spiritual Laws*
1957	The Cat in the Hat published
1961	Berlin Wall built
	Soviets launch first man in space
1962	Campus crusade moves to Arrowhead springs
1967	First heart transplant
1968	Martin Luther King assassinated
1969	Neil Armstrong first man on the moon
1970	Computer floppy disks introduced
1971	United Kingdom changes to decimal system for currency
1973	Picasso dies
1979	Jesus film launched
1980	Olympic games held in Moscow
1981	First woman appointed to U.S. supreme court
1983	The Year of the Bible
1986	Challenger space shuttle explodes
1989	Berlin Wall falls
1991	Collapse of the Soviet Union
	South Africa appeals apartheid laws
1996	Bill Bright awarded Templeton Prize for Progress in Religion
1997	Hong Kong returned to China
1999	Panama canal returns to Panama
2000	Year of the Millennium
2001	Twin towers attacks 09/11
2003	Bill Bright dies

CHRISTIAN FOCUS

Staying faithful - Reaching out!

Christian Focus Publications publishes books for adults and children under its three main imprints: Christian Focus, Mentor and Christian Heritage. Our books reflect that God's word is reliable and Jesus is the way to know him, and live for ever with him.

Our children's publication list includes a Sunday school curriculum that covers pre-school to early teens; puzzle and activity books. We also publish personal and family devotional titles, biographies and inspirational stories that children will love.

If you are looking for quality Bible teaching for children then we have an excellent range of Bible story and age specific theological books.

From pre-school to teenage fiction, we have it covered!

Find us at our web page:
www.christianfocus.com